Laughter Effects

By

Sandra Moulin

ISBN: 9798676223540

Table of Contents

Author

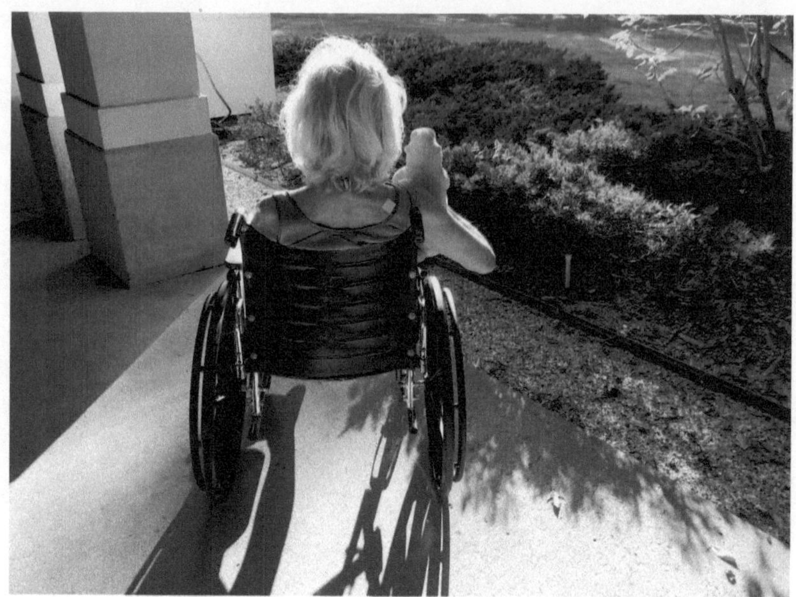

On November 9, 2019, my life was changed forever. As I was taking my daily 3.5 mile walk in our beautiful suburban neighborhood, I was struck by a truck at a crosswalk and thrown into the air, landing very hard on my left side. As I lay on the ground, wondering what had happened, all I could think of was whether I would ever be able to walk or even play the piano again.

I was airlifted to the Trauma Unit at our local hospital where the surgeon announced to my husband prior to surgery: "I am just trying to save her foot, and the rest is up to God". There was nothing funny about this, nor was there any humor in the injuries from which I am still healing three quarters of a year later. There was, however, an opportunity for me to embrace the pain and find a way to cope with this tragedy. My way was humor. I had to immediately go into survival mode, and laughter and silly were my inspiration.

I joked with the aids and chuckled at how ridiculous I looked all wrapped up in casts and stuck with tubes. When I was finally able to sit in a wheelchair, I made sure to put a stiletto on the good foot and a bow in my matted hair. I shared my hospital bed with a small stuffed Prairie Dog (P.D.) who made me laugh every morning when I woke up to the wtf expression on his little face. I wrote blogs from my hospital bed, and I spoke French with the Haitian woman who cleaned my room. I had Mr. Wonderful take pictures of the magic wand sent by a dear friend and the red sequined "Dorothy" slippers that my daughter sent me. Sometimes I had to force myself to laugh so I wouldn't sob. It was a surreal experience, and when, after months of therapy, I took my first steps again, Mr. Wonderful caught it all on camera and cried.

When I arrived home on December 1, still in my wheelchair, I had no idea that only a few months later, we would be faced with a life-altering global pandemic which would force me to stay at home indefinitely. Four very long months after the accident, however, following extensive physical therapy, I was walking two miles a day and riding my bike to breakfast with my husband. I could not have gotten to that point without the love and support of my incredibly patient and loving husband, my wonderful, devoted daughters and the overwhelming generous caring of so many friends. There were tears, but there was also laughter. I made an unconscious decision to celebrate the healing instead of focusing on what I perhaps had lost. Humor heals. It led me to a place of gratitude, and that is the predominant emotion that lingers with me to this day.

When I stroll around the house practicing walking in my stilettos, there is a huge grin on my face. When I can play a Rachmaninov passage almost perfectly, I am filled with joy and humbled by what I have learned about the daily gift of life, standing on my own two feet and playing a melody that fills my heart.

July 8, 2020
Sandra Moulin

Chapter 1: Domestic

"*I love being married. It's so great to
find that one special person you want to
annoy for the rest of your life.*"

Rita Rudner

Dear Diary

Today, I will confess all my secrets. By doing this, I will purge myself of the guilt associated with them, and my sleepless nights will end.

1. I ate the last cookie in the jar in 1948.
2. I lied about my homework in 1953.
3. I wrote on Peter K's pink shirt in fourth grade.
4. I crumbled my graham cracker on my closet floor when I was mad at Daddy.
5. I got a D in Anthropology.
6. I gossiped.
7. I read Mom's Peyton Place dog-eared pages.
8. I tried on Mommy's dentures.
9. I tried to pee like Daddy.
10. I thought a condom was a place to live.

The "She Shed"

There are many ways to decorate the new "She Shed." Mine is on order. Here is my list of furnishings:

1. Ryan Gosling
2. George Clooney
3. Matthew McConaughey
4. Tom Brady
5. Andrea Bocelli
6. The Marlboro Man
7. Justin Timberlake
8. Clark Gable blow-up doll
9. Chris Hemsworth
10. Antonio Banderas

Cleaning Persons

It may come as a shock to some that a retiree would consider hiring cleaning persons. I have had such a person in the past, but my experience was less than stellar. The first one was so hot that Mr. Wonderful followed her around the house claiming to explain things to her, when she and I both knew he was just drooling over her fine tush (is that a word?)

The second one smelled of cigarette smoke and proceeded to suck up the fringe of our expensive oriental rug into our brand new vacuum cleaner. She didn't last long, neither did the vacuum cleaner.

The final one whined the whole time, claiming she didn't get two degrees to be on her knees scrubbing grout. That would have been me.

So why would someone who has no full-time job need to hire cleaning people? Lord knows, retirees must have a lot of time to do such things. Well, guess what, gentlemen? You all decided that trimming the bushes, raking the leaves and mowing the lawn were no longer fun. We ladies are sick of cleaning the fridge and scrubbing the shower stalls. Can we do it? Do we have time? Of course. We just don't want to.

I have figured out after much financial juggling that I can do without goat cheese and fruit for a month to pay for someone to make my tile sparkle. Stay tuned. Mr. Wonderful magnanimously acquiesced saying, "You pay for it, you go for it."

Classified

WANTED:

1. Hot hubby who does dishes and pays for cleaning lady.
2. Resident 10-year-old to manage technology.
3. Resident handyman who will hang pictures within two years of asking.
4. Personal shopper to find bargains at Saks and Neimans and pay for them.
5. Personal florist to deliver bouquets and sign them from hot celebs.
6. Personal photographer to get me from angles which make me look like a bodybuilder or a playboy bunny.
7. Resident male trainer 25-28.
8. Resident reader to read all my Book Club books, give me a 3-sentence synopsis and write three intelligent questions to take to the meeting.
9. A grandma.
10. Monthly sex-toy. (See Page 208)

Budget, Fudge it!

The budget. Before retirement, we didn't need a budget. We had money. Before retirement, a budget was what you did with your time, not your finances. After twelve years on "the budget," I'm here to say, it sucks. Having a budget means I have to reveal how I manage my money. This has always been a very private, secret, sacred part of my existence. To reveal such intimate information (as well as the private stash) was unsettling from the start and continues to be.

Although, I realize there are people who can somehow take this page and find out how much money we don't make through some shifty techno talent, I will not reveal details of the budget. I will only suggest ways of fudging the budget. Savvy women know that having your own secret stash is the only way to survive and thrive in the world of fashion and frolic.

I have two, count 'em, two piggy banks. Mr. Wonderful laughs. Let him chuckle while I cash in my quarter rolls for $732.25—enough to buy my "if-I-get-mad-ticket-to-Tahiti." There is freedom and power in the piggy. The small piggy bank houses the nickels and dimes. This one doesn't offer quite the punch, but I can purchase a pair of pants with this pork.

The only control I have over the budget is how much I allot to the grocery category. I usually suggest at least $1000/month. He questions this, but I tell him that if he wants to continue his magic menu of Raisin Bran and prunes, he must support Post cereals and prune farms. This is not cheap. Still not convinced, he might muster the courage to ask how much I spent on the last shopping. I will reply, "Well, your Cranberry Juice went up to $4.79 a bottle, and your Gluten Free diet has caused a 36% increase in the food budget." That pretty much shuts him up.

The point is that by saving a major percentage of the grocery budget, I am able to "fudge it" and fill up my closet with oink bargains.

Mind Reading

Before dating a guy, we should ask him if he likes to read. He will most often say, "yes," or "yes, it depends." (If he's a lawyer, everything depends, until he has to wear them). Once he has stated that he likes to read, he has no excuse not to read our minds. We are open books, after all, and men are often unreadable. The reason they are unreadable is that there's no content in there. They are not thinking, reflecting, plotting, debating like we are 24/7; they are simply sitting there. It took me almost twenty years to figure that one out, ladies, so waste no more time; there is no Table of Contents for men. They are just one simple chapter that has no plot, no conflicts to resolve, no theme, no climax (the latter depends on the man). We, au contraire, are open books.

Why can't they read our minds? They said "Yes," they like to read. So what's the problem? When he asks, "What's wrong?" and we say "Nothing," lips pursed, why can't they read our minds? "Nothing" means at minimum "something," and usually "everything." When he asks, "Would you like a vacuum cleaner for our anniversary?" Do not be surprised that he is not reading your mind. He honestly thinks because you said three years ago last Wednesday, "Boy, I could use a new vacuum cleaner," that you really want one. He will look at your scrunched-up face and seriously not be able to translate. To you, it may be very clear that the Tiffany necklace was the priority, but to him, you never came right out and said, "I would like that Tiffany necklace, right there." You must give him a sticky note with the style number, and you must program the GPS accordingly. Do not put the price on said sticky. This is self-defeating. Men love surprises.

The Quintessential Christmas Letter

Dear Friends:

Since last year, our life has been a real roller coaster. From Jimmy's National Merit Scholarship designation and ceremony to Bob's getting promoted and transferred to a Penthouse office in Paris, it has been one thing after another.

Megan's husband was transferred to San Diego with Google so she and the twins followed him out there last month, and they've just moved into their cliff-side home. We pray the four dogs don't end up in the ocean below. One of them had puppies the day they closed, so she's been somewhat fussy lately (the dog, well, actually she and the dog).

Kevin's parents have moved to a Senior Facility, and they love it, but his mom is jealous of all the women who are after Charlie. She says they fight over who will dance with him at the weekly cotillion. He's been known to disappear at 5:00, and she suspects he's down the hall in Mabel's room.

I've just finished my third Iron Woman race. I came in first in my age category, so I was pretty hyped. Unfortunately, I knocked over two competitors on the way, so they're threatening to take away my medal. Stupid bitches were in my way.

The baby is teething, so sleep is sporadic at best. I've tried everything to get her to sleep through the night including Chopra meditation tapes, but nothing seems to work. The bags under my eyes are the size of grapefruits. I tried cucumbers, but I need about nine slices per eye, and I can't hold them on my face and juggle nursing the baby at the same time. Maybe she needs to be weaned.

My job has been hell lately. They want to promote me to Vice President, but I'm just so busy juggling my Iron Woman training, the baby, the move to France, and skyping my high school sweetheart who just surfaced (and is he ever hot!), I don't know if I can take on one more thing. It would be nice to wear that badge, however.

Well, I hope this letter finds you all healthy and thriving like us. It's a "Wonderful Life" here in the Hamptons. Vive la France.

Love,

Mary

P.S. My mother recently married the Mayor of Poughkeepsie. He's 38.

Snore

Once upon a time two newlyweds round two
had so many blessings, oh, what could they do?
Enjoy them, be grateful, start a new life together
But what kind of pillow? Foam or some feather?

The bed was quite old, so a new one they bought
a topper for his bed? No, that one she fought.
The thing was like dough
it left an imprint
of her small, shapely body.
He didn't take the hint.

Then noises resounded in the middle of the night
they started and stopped and gave her a fright
"What's that?" she gasped, looking around
It was her hubby. Oh no! She was stuck with the sound.

Night after night, she tried to sleep through
he snorted and whistled, oh, what could she do?
These blessings were hidden beneath his sweet smile
She gritted her teeth and made do for a while.

Years passed so quickly. Great fun they enjoyed.
But sounds kept on coming, and she got quite annoyed.
"I want just one night of quiet and rest."
Accepting her fate, four hours at best.

Trying the pillows over her head
She tried the noise maker next to her bed
"No help!" she whined to her family and friends
They all rolled their eyes and giggled instead.

Nose strips and ear plugs, nothing would work
soon, she began to call him a jerk
This was not healthy for a marriage so sweet
She even considered putting him out on the street.

Finally, her patience gave out and in tears
she moved to the guest room, first time in years
"I must get my rest. My nerves are all frayed.
Don't have to sleep with him just to get . . . "

Now they are happy, two seniors in sync
They get ready for bed after one tiny drink
He purrs in his pillow, all happy alone
She reads in her bedroom, white noise on her phone.

What price must we pay for a nighttime of mellow?
After all he is quite a kindly old fellow
He loves her so deeply and regrets his snore flaw
She loves him too, but is pleased with no "saw."

Fifteen Candles

I am convinced there is a light-bulb conspiracy. Three-way bulbs are really only two-way. Yup. The first setting, the warm, cozy, curl-up-in-a-ball-read-a-book-setting lasts about 72 hours and then it's gone. What is this? You pay for three ways, and you only get two? To whom does one complain? I know Edison has been gone for some time. There is no "bulb-buddy" app or specialist at the stores. You can't even ask a question about light bulbs at a store anymore. The bulbs are back in the Jockey short section of most box stores. I guess the promoters are trying to light up the package.

I have friends who say our home is like coming to a cave. This is probably true. I like it dim and cozy. I only turn the two-way to the first super bright setting when I'm absolutely desperate to locate the curly fry I dropped on the floor, or when I am attempting to decipher a number in the phone book, now the size of a book of matches. (I guess people don't use phones or phone books anymore.)

I try to use candles when we have dinner parties, but Mr. Wonderful claims he's allergic to the wax. What? He isn't allergic to the candle in the bedroom, so why is he allergic to the ones on the dining room table? Hmm. I know. I'm going to trick him. I will bring the bedroom candle to the dining room table when he's not looking and see what happens.

Just Breathe

Of all the things I've learned in the years on this planet, I neglected one important lesson: breathe. Yes, I discovered recently that I conduct most of my daily business holding my breath. I can't even count how many times people in my life have said to me, "Just breathe." Like, you think I don't know how to breathe? Are you effen kidding me? Well, guess what? They were right. I don't breathe. Breathing is such a waste of time, and time is precious. Who knows from one day to the next if we're going to get hit by a meteor or shot by a psychopath? Breathing is over-rated.

I've recently tried to meditate to help me slow down the mental calisthenics I apparently perform 24/7. Meditation will do it, if you can sit still long enough and actually inhale and exhale more than once. Meditation to me is like putting myself on a treadmill and turning it on at .1 mph. I figure if I hurry up and get my meditating over with, I can move on down my "To Do" list faster, and I'll feel so good about breathing. Nope. It doesn't work that way.

Meditating teaches us to let go of the extraneous and focus on the joy of the now. What? I don't get the now. Now is one of those fleeting sensations like orgasms. It feels fab, and then suddenly it's gone. Why would you spend all that effort on something that fleets?

The great meditators are dead. Socrates, Ghandi, Plato, Joseph, Nixon. Shows you what meditating did for them.

My new Chopra Meditation program is supposed to be great. I have nine days of the program saved in my "OPEN" file. Once I get to the "now," I'll listen to them. Maybe I'll have time this afternoon. So I will deal with the now then.

Who remembers the guy who wrote the book, "The Power of Now?" See, proves my point. He's already at then, and no one remembers his name.

Being Right

How important is being right to you? I would like to say, "It doesn't really matter." I would be lying. When Mr. Wonderful thinks he's right, and I know he's wrong, some second grade mechanism in my brain goes berserk, and I will want to explain to my death how it's impossible for me to be wrong. That was how it used to be, until I realized one day that no one wins when someone has to be right. The worst conversation about being right is the one you have in public.

Last night, we were out for dinner. Mr. Wonderful ordered the dish that I had ordered the previous time. I couldn't even eat it; it was so bad. He ordered it anyway against my recommendation. (He likes to show me that I am not the boss of him).

He ordered it, and, of course, he didn't like it. I ordered a wonderful Arctic Char that had a little crust on it from some light pan searing. He said, "You have the same crust on your fish that I have on this casserole." I said, "No, this is different. This isn't bread crumbs like yours; it's just a coating to make it a little crisp." He continued to argue with me in front of a new member of our dining group. I let it go. He continued. The waiter arrived, and Mr. W. asked, "Is that topping the same as mine?" The waiter said, "No, sir. Hers is a blah blah blah." Flummoxed, Mr. Wonderful said, "Ok. I'm sorry. I was wrong."

(This has only happened about three times in the past 24.6 years.)

Now I could have left it there. But I didn't. The waiter was not describing the crust; he was describing the dollop of sauce on the top of the crust, so he clearly misunderstood the question. I could have just let Mr. Wonderful think he was wrong, but instead, I humbly and lovingly said, "He didn't understand your question. He was talking about what was on top of the crust." I did this because it was true and because I didn't want Mr. Wonderful to be wrong in front of others. Unfortunately, I was not given the same consideration.

These are "I'm-right-and-I'll-prove-it" discussions that belong behind closed doors. Did I bring it up later? No. Why? Because it's a battle I choose not to fight. There are battles that are worth my blood and others that are just too stupid. Crust, no crust, crumbs—who the hell cares? Being right? Is that really what matters? It's never about what it's about.

Cooking

Cooking. What is this? My mother taught me how to make pork chops and scalloped potatoes in 1958. I don't think that qualifies. The pork chops tasted good then, but when I have tried this same recipe at least 47 times over the past 56 years, they never seem to taste the same. They are dry, and the flour on the potatoes doesn't blend, so the dish looks like clumps of snow-sprinkled cow patties.

I have never really aspired to being a "cook." Cooking to me is for people who eat. I don't eat. I pick. I pick one thing on the plate that looks pretty, and I dissect it slowly. The rest, I push around so it looks used. How is that an inspiration to spend hours searching for recipes, weeks shopping for ingredients, and days preparing a meal? Not my gig.

The problem with not cooking is that it's hard to entertain. If you invite people to your home for dinner, they expect you to cook. That sucks. I thought I had the issue resolved when Mr. Wonderful got his brand new shiny grill. He could be in charge of the main dish, and all I'd have to do is tear up some lettuce, put some veggies in a bag in the micro and buy multiple bottles of wine when Walgreens had their BOGO. But no. Mr. Wonderful was not buying the "I'm-in-charge-of-the-dinner-party" gig. So, back to the burner I go.

After my first disastrous dinner party a year ago, I've shied away from the whole entertaining thing. I made my one and only "made-this-twenty-times" recipe. One woman passed the dish, and said, "No. I don't want any." Her husband took a piece of my fabulous salmon. It was the size of a bar of soap from the Hampton Inn. Two others were vegans, so they brought their own casserole, which looked disgusting. Needless to say, it was an evening not to remember.

As I am very resilient, I thought, "Maybe I should take some cooking classes at the Publix Cooking School." I only had this thought once, and I've recovered. No more "Bon Appétit" for moi.

Man's Journal

Got up. Took dump. Read paper. Checked Weather. Windy and humid. To do list: gas and wash cars.

Played tennis. Took nap. Ate lunch. Checked off things on to do list. Took nap.

Wrote emails. Paid a couple of bills. Looked for glasses. Found glasses. Took nap.

Ate dinner. Washed dishes. Took nap. Watched car program. Good day. Went to bed.

Polite Sucks

I often marvel at how much time people spend listening to recipes they never intend to try, directions to locations they never plan to visit, entrée specials that make them gag and stories that seem to have no ending or point. I've concluded that I am too polite, and I need to come up with a kind way of saying, "I really don't give a damn."

Yesterday, we were having breakfast at our B & B when a woman began telling us about a sailing excursion she and her husband enjoyed. We have no intention of ever taking this trip, but because we are Mr. and Mrs. Polite, we listened attentively. The lady went on and on about the box lunch, the blue sky, the captain's hilarious pirate stories, the clean restrooms and the nice couple they met from Iowa. Mr. Wonderful, being even more polite than moi, just had to ask a question. This is rule number one: Do not, I repeat, do not ask questions when you are already uninterested and bored. This simply gave the woman license to go off on a ten-minute tangent about the ship's history.

People also get stuck in this situation at restaurants when the waitperson launches into the daily specials. What really annoys me is the introduction, "This is my all-time favorite. I just love it!" What do we care what this person loves? We don't even know her? We love the purple-snouted platypus, but we're not asking her to pet one. Anyway, she stands up tall to recite her shtick about the entrée of the day. "The chef has prepared a short-rib that he has slow-cooked for twelve days. He has added to this some fish scales, a quarter pound of garlic and some hummus balls. He is offering it this evening accompanied by a side of cheese grits and a tomato slice." Boy, we sure can't wait to try this. The young woman is so proud that she has remembered her whole spiel in one breath that she has to reach down and touch her toes to restore her oxygen. I say, "I'll just have the burger and fries, please. Hold the gristle."

Sometimes when people are telling us about a restaurant they frequent because the food is so good, but "there is no ambiance," I have already tuned out before realizing that they are going to do a New York Times restaurant review complete with specific directions. I just want to give them the time out sign, but Mr. Wonderful has already politely smiled encouraging them to take the stage for their soliloquy. I have never eaten at a restaurant just because the food was good. Who does that? If there's no ambiance, I might as well cook a filet and eat it in the laundry room.

In France, they say, "A chacun son goût." (To each his own.) My own is my own, and I make it a practice not to force it on anyone else. Hello.

Downsizing

When you decide to downsize, be careful what you wish for. These are not on the list:

1. Important parts of male anatomy
2. Important parts of female anatomy
3. Closets
4. Basements
5. Attics
6. Garages
7. Budgets
8. Bar
9. Female ego.
10. Mad money

Recently, we downsized our home. Moving from 3000 square feet to 900 is like going from a size 7 shoe to a size 4 narrow. Are you effen kidding me? I can't find half my clothes because I've had to store some of them in the pantry next to the dry mustard. I can't find my curling iron because I think he put it in the toolbox, which hasn't been seen since the movers took off with our couch.

I have yet to locate my négligées. It's not that I wear them; it's just nice being able to tell myself I can still get into them (or out of them, as the case may be).

He can't find his good socks. I think I used them to stuff the crystal box to avoid breakage. I hope our liqueur glasses don't smell like a locker room.

We only have room for one sauté pan. As I have never sautéed, it's no great loss, but I was planning on making a pie in that thing.

The measuring cups disappeared. I really needed those to figure out how much vodka to put in my Cosmo. Oh, I forgot, I don't drink. Well, at least not so anyone would notice.

Speaking of Cosmo, I haven't seen that magazine collection. Takes me back and aback.

Good Vibrations

One of the more recent additions to the nail salon is the vibrating chair. Some nail artists give the customer a choice. Others flip the switch, maybe to keep the client from trying to tell her life story. You really can't talk when this chair is shaking every part of your anatomy. You're doing your best to hold still so you don't end up with polish on your proboscis.

The first time I experienced the vibrating chair, my lips broke into the letter O. The sensation I was feeling in my back gradually wormed its way down my spine into my buttocks. I never had this feeling in daylight. The seat of the chair actually seemed to rise under me, and the back of the seat pushed me forward until I had to hang on so as not to fall into the exfoliant. The O spread into an AH, and I quickly realized that I needed to get a grip. The knuckle-like kneading released all tension from my body, and I soon found myself eyesclosed, lips moistened, fantasizing about nude beaches in St. Barts. Somewhere in the distance, I heard a voice. It became louder. I opened my eyes and saw the nice man on the stool below trying to get my attention. "Do you want same color on nails?" "Ah, O, yes, that would be fine," I purred.

Wanted: Politian Who

1. doesn't need a GPS to cross the aisle.
2. doesn't Tweet.
3. doesn't grab women's cheeks.
4. has scruples.
5. hears constituents.
6. acts on what he hears.
7. has balls.
8. doesn't use balls with enTitleist on them.
9. checks with what his spouse is saying and doing.
10. owns own shit.

Pop Art

I read recently in a pop psychology magazine that in many cities in the world, there are sweet, loving wives sitting at the breakfast table taking their spouse's crap. They are pissed off and feeling powerless. But they are not. They are not powerless. They have power that no man wants to mess with: the POP, the Power of the Pan. (Had you going there for a second, didn't I?)

Women who feel voiceless can do any of the following to maintain equilibrium in a relationship:

1.   refuse to cook
2.   cook badly
3.   order out nightly
4.   disappear right before dinner
5.   pepper all food heavily
6.   fold in some vodka balls*

There are always creative solutions to any problem. Unfortunately, one can't always think of them until after the fact. Perhaps if women kept a "POP" file, they could run to the file cabinet in the middle of a confrontation, and voilà, playing field leveled.

*Mr. Wonderful read this and said, "I didn't know vodka had balls."

Sleep Apnea

A dear couple we know informed us recently that they both have sleep apnea. In order to prevent a major physical trauma by the cessation of their breathing, they just wear plastic masks over their faces at night. These things look like large oxygen masks. They cover not just the mouth but half of each cheek.

This begs the question of how they manage foreplay. Lord knows, they don't want to have a stroke at the ultimate moment of erotic pleasure. So how do they kiss or whisper sweet nothings when their lips are covered in plastic?

Depending on the position (of the mask), it must be weird to be staring at each other with six inches of plastic between their faces. How do they not laugh? How do they not get fogged up? What happens to the moan? Does it get stuck in the mask and then become recycled into a grunt?

This gives a whole new meaning to oral sex. I wonder if there is an app for this.

Please Leave Me:

1. Your legs: Tina Turner
2. Your voice: Josh Groban
3. Your compassion: Mother Theresa
4. Your courage: Gabby Giffords
5. Your resilience: Jackie Robinson
6. Your integrity: Abe Lincoln
7. Your humility: Pope Francis
8. Your tenacity: Lindsay Vonn
9. Your money: Oprah Winfrey
10. Your hair: Eva Longoria
11. Your body: Jessica Alba
12. Your athletic ability: Serena Williams
13. Your talent: Hugh Jackman
14. Your arms: Jillian Michaels
15. Your house: Kate Middleton
16. Your wisdom: The Dali Lama
17. Your sense of humor: Dave Barry

Just imagine what I could do, if I had any combination of these traits. I could sing my way to England in my private "O" jet and sign my humor books in my royal mansion.

I could toss my gorgeous locks and show off my six-pack and arm muscles while skiing down the Alps in a cast.

I could offer my wisdom while dancing across the stage delivering an incredible drop shot.

OR

I could kiss babies and pray for the sick while planking on the battlefield.

I could flaunt my flawless body while bringing in three runs.

The possibilities are endless.

The Thermostat

I hereby proclaim that the thermostat is assigned to the female of the household. Men do not understand heat. They have not been in it or soaked through their nightshirts from it. They are out of touch to the highest degree. The only "heat" they understand is the one they're in. Forget the Pre-nup, ladies. You are much better off with the Pre-heat contract. Just think how controlling their temperature empowers us.

The Four Commandments of Household Temperature:

1. Thou shalt leave thermostat wherever woman sets it.
2. Thou shalt not change thermostat when woman is out of house.
3. Thou shalt not whine about household temperature.
4. Thou shalt put up screens, build fire or don hunting shirt to cope with woman's setting.

It has been reported that a mischievous husband from Rebuke, Iowa, tried to change the household thermostat. He was last seen shirtless hitchhiking to Punta Gorda with only a small backpack and a lukewarm beer.

Gardening 101

Who knew I would be gardening in my seventies. Well, "gardening" is a very loose term in this household. It means watering the 20-some plants we bought from the previous owners and watching the bougainvilleas in the front of our house wilt and die.

I am not a gardener. Gardening is for people who like to feel the earth, get a sense of worms and dirt—feel the joy of a bloom. For me, the earth is best felt underneath my stilettos, dirt is non-negotiable, and blooms are things Mr. Wonderful should be sending me and isn't.

These twenty-some plants that we purchased from the previous owners for $150 including pots are one royal pain in my buttocks. I didn't want them, but I was persuaded that if we didn't buy them, it would cost hundreds of dollars to replace them. This is true, but the argument was based on the false assumption that I wanted plants. Watering these puppies is simply annoying. One day they look fabulous, the next, they're wilting in defiance. As they sit around our lovely pool, when the wind picks up, the large leaves love to dance along the pool surface so someone has to go scoop them out. That's the pool guy's job, but he only comes once a week.

Speaking of the pool guy, I thought he was supposed to be a movie star type. I didn't count on a squat fur-faced Amish man. What do you want for $15 a month?

The bougainvilleas are the most annoying. They thrive on drought. What? Yes, the nice landscape guy said the reason they were dying was that they were getting too much water. This seems counter-intuitive to me, but what do I know? I play the piano.

I used to have several indoor plants, but Mr. Wonderful got tired of listening to me whine about how long it took to water them, so I buy flowers once a month to add life to the interior of our tiny jewel. Sometimes I put a card with them—a gentle hint that maybe someone else sent them to me, but he's on to that one. I guess I'm just going to have to suck it up with succulents.

Chapter 11: Body Image

"... and I said to my body, softly, 'I want to be your friend.' It took a long breath and replied, 'I have been waiting my whole life for this.'"

Sally Anon

Collagen Fairy

Somewhere between the time of conception and delivery, the Collagen Fairy sneaks into the womb and distributes the female child's ration of collagen. The Fairy is a woman because men don't even think about this stuff, and women who are universally and historically threatened by one another know that your lifetime supply is never the same as that of your sisters.

She randomly doles out this golden substance, and it's not until the woman is approaching fifty that she begins to realize that this Collagen Chic was either a saint or the devil herself. Yes, not all of us have equal amounts. There were never laws that dictated how much collagen each of us would receive, and we can't get refills, ladies. No amendment to the Constitution will help you once this stuff begins to disappear.

You can massage your skin, apply numerous "miracle" creams, have your cheeks injected with cow dung—nothing will bring the collagen back; so don't let anyone fool you. It was that Collagen Biatch who decided your fate. You either look like Jennifer Aniston until you're 90, or you're screwed.

Itch Over The Upper Thigh

Do guys really think we don't notice them rearranging their body parts? I would love to know what they would think if we did the same.

Think about the baseball players and what they do while they're winding up. And what about a certain tennis pro whose visible jock line always seems to get displaced during his serve. He's got the whole shtick down pat: rock back and forth, push hair behind ear, dig fabric out of ass.

What if women went around reaching into their dresses and fondling their tatas? What if we scratched where it itched every time the sensation demanded it? What if we walked by some hot dude and let it rip? The world would be a much cruder place. Would men even notice?

What About Big Wigs?

Every woman should have a "do" she can slap on for the vacay. A "do" that DOes itself, that doesn't require washing, drying, volumizing, productizing, curling or straightening. This is particularly true of those of us who spend 29 days a month in a convertible. Besides the issue of horizontal windburn streaks across our cheeks and mulch in our molars, we need to do something about the top-down-hair-conundrum.

I suppose there are wigs one can buy, but then there's the issue of them flying off into a marsh or sinkhole en route. I'm told wigs are hot, and when Mr. Wonderful is driving at the speed of sound, I don't need any more sweat to clog my follicles.

Supposedly, some genius has invented shoes that tie themselves, so why can't some brilliant woman come up with a cool wig that doesn't mat down the original tresses, that fits ergonomically on any pate and makes us look like Angelina ready to walk down the red carpet when we descend from the two-seater?

In the meantime, I am doing my hair six times a day: first thing in the morning when I can't even see my reflection, two hours later when I can, after completing the morning's errands, before going to the trendy beach lunch spot, after the 4:00 nap when I can't see my reflection again, and finally, before going to the sexy nightclub on the water.

This is overkill, and by the end of the day, my products are half-empty, and my hair looks like a cement helmet, my face moving freely underneath.

I could just cut it short like a boy, but this is a last resort for me. I still like the perks that come with being a sensuous long-haired "mature" blond: jerking my head just slightly to the right so my waves sway in slow motion, the feel of locks on my shoulders to remind myself that I still have enough hair to reach them, the ability to pull a few tresses across my left eye to give me the "sultry" look, and the status symbol of owning a comb and roll brush—something I took for granted the first six decades of my life. Besides, what would we do without Drano?

Hair today, gone tomorrow.

Skin

I hate my skin. It's not like you can do anything about it. If you don't like your hair, you can color it, cut it, perm it, highlight it, or wear a hat. With skin, there's nothing you can do.

I have a friend who's always showing me how great her skin is. "I have great arms," she always brags. I just want to tell her to wrap those friggin' arms around herself and feel the love—the love she obviously feels for herself.

As my skin ages, it is so thin, you can see the blood rushing through my veins. I have so many barnacles I might as well just open a museum and put myself on display. "Can we count the spots and bumps, boys and girls?"

I've always been "thin-skinned," but this is ridiculous. if I scratch an itch, there's a bruise. When the bruise finally goes away, maybe three or four weeks later, it leaves an unsightly mark. My grandchildren could play connect the dots for a month with my collection.

Wouldn't it be lovely if we could just unzip our skin and trade it for someone else's? The problem with that is that their skin comes with their flaws, their problems, their insecurities, their genes and their attitudes. Do we really want to trade a few barnacles for a damaged ship?

A Farewell To Arms

When you were a little girl, you probably never thought about your arms. Arms were for hugging grandpas, carrying baby dolls, stretching as tall as you can and flying like a bird.

When you grow into a young girl, arms become flailing mechanisms for football-game-cheering and throwing hissy fits at your mother. An unpleasant odor begins to escape from the pit, so you rub scent-free stuff to hide the smell and keep your arms close to your body "just in case."

Once you are a full-blown teen, arms become embracing vehicles for boyfriends and bffs. They have been known to nail an overhead, elbow younger siblings and balance books and backpacks.

At the point that you realize that arms now represent a part of the female anatomy that attracts potential life partners, arm-toning becomes part of the weekly body sculpting routine. Years ago, the 35-24-35 figure never focused on arms, but times have changed.

Beautifully-sculpted arms are now a "given" in the "what-a-body!" image.

By the time, I figured it all out, mine had creped-out. Yup, I've got plenty of muscle tone in each bicep, tricep, whatever-cep, but it's all surrounded by crepe, so now I'm supposed to hide them. No way. Crepe, crap, I refuse to say "Farewell."

What A Waist!

I have often wondered about what a waist should look like? Should there be exactly ten inches less in one's waist than in one's bust line? Is there a requirement for movie stars, models, factory workers?

I have never had a waist. No, never. I was not born with one, and no matter how many Christmas lists I put it on, Santa never delivered. There were occasional hints on and off through the years, but pregnancy and apple strudel squelched that fantasy.

It really isn't the waist that's the issue. The real issue is the size of the bust and the hips in relationship to the waist. If both are large, then the waist appears small even if it isn't. Great. Now all I have to do is get a boob job and go to Brazil for a year, and I've got the waist thing licked. (Do not lick the waist. This is bad for the neck).

Less Is Less, More Or Less

Less is less. Whoever said less is more isn't dealing with more of less. For those of us who had more and now have less, we are dealing with a seriously troubling phenomenon: less of what matters.

For all of you out there with your signs of who and what matters, here's what matters:

HAIR Matters

COLLAGEN matters

EYELASHES matter

ORGANS matter

SEX matters

TEETH and GUMS matter

MEMORY matters

I had much hair. Now I have wisps.
I had cheeks. Now I have pouches.
I had eyelashes. Now I have two or three
strands of feckless fringe.
I had organs. Now I have orgs.
I think I had sex, but I can't remember.
I had teeth, but they are receding into my
gums. No one has seen then for a while.
I had memory, or did I?

Less is not more. Less is effen less. Let's be clear. This was not a choice. I choose more.

Chapter III: Technology

"Technology makes it possible for people to gain control over every- thing, except technology."

John Tudor

Techno-Talk

Like computers, there should be some key understanding between partners. The terminology used by both parties must be easily understood and mastered. Here are a few basic keys to a successful relationship.

1. When things aren't going well, SHIFT.
2. When there is conflict, the CONTROL factor is usually the culprit.
3. Try COMMAND to get your way. If that doesn't work, ESCAPE.
4. When you RETURN, think about OPTIONS.
5. When bad things emerge from your pie hole, DELETE.

Locked In A Cell

Who ever thought of a phone as a prison? It is. I am locked in this prison more hours a day than I choose to admit. Et tu, Brutus? How many of us ever thought we'd be locked in this cell multiple hours per day? I thought I could go one day without it, but I can't. I'm addicted.

My name is Fifi, la Folle, and I am a technoholic. I spend more hours with my devices than I do cleaning the house (that's a no-brainer), organizing my life, primping (that's huge), cooking (?), working out, writing my book, practicing my piano, even thinking. The question is what did I used to do with these hours, and when am I doing those things now?

My phone is a cell—a prison where I have the key, but I don't even use it. I lock myself in here everyday, and I never utter a word. My fingers do the talking, so they don't even have to articulate, speak up, breathe or even use proper grammar. If I choose, I don't have to utter a single word for days at a time. Maybe the next time one of those obnoxious wine-fogged women starts flapping her jaw, I should just hand her a phone.

How many of us realize that we are walking around carrying our autobiographies in our pockets? If you read anyone's phone, you will find out everything you need to know about him or her and stuff you don't. If employers want to weed out the psychos from their job applicants, forget the application process, just read their phones. Probably 25-50% of the people applying would be jobless. Is there anything on your phone you wouldn't want people to see or read?

If I were my parent, I'd ground me. I'd make me sit in my room for several hours with no devices. I would make me talk for at least 30 minutes. That would almost kill me. I would tell me that until I could write (in legible cursive) how I am going to limit my screen time to no more than 45 minutes per day, I would not be allowed out of my room, and I could have no molasses cookies. (That's a real game-changer.) I would not allow me to take the phone out of the house.

Someone needs to write a 12-step plan for technoholics. They could make it an app, so we would find it easy to follow. It would go something like this:

Day 1: Set timer on app to determine how much time you spend per day on this device.

Day 2: Punish self for spending so much time on device.

Day 3: Reward self for trying to reduce hours spent on device.

Day 4: Put device in drawer for a minimum of one hour per day.

Day 5: Drink.

Day 6: Reward self for keeping device in drawer for one hour. Now triple that.

Day 7: Buy gift for self for accomplishing step 6.

Day 8:   Apologize to all the people you've ignored while being on device.

Day 9:   Knew you needed more than one day for 8.

Day 10:   Keep device in drawer at least five hours.

Day 11:   Cry, pound floor with fists, jump rope (do not use for other purpose), whisper bad words.

Day 12:   You did it. Take that puppy out, and send yourself a congratulations message. You're not addicted; you're just in love.

The Gif Of Life

What is a Gif? A gift without the "t?" Seniors aren't always privy to the trends of the mainstream. A Gif is a moving cartoonish concept that people use on social media to make a point. For the older generation, such new things are fascinating. I'm sure young people on Facebook are laughing hysterically when they see anyone over 50 posting a Gif.

You can't illustrate a Gif in a book. It does make one wonder, however, who comes up with this stuff. Why wasn't it you or me? We could have been millionaires by now. But no. We had ridiculous ideas like these (the pet rock, the pot holder), but we didn't act on our idea. We probably thought, "Who would want one of those?" Only three million Americans and a handful of Russians.

Did you know that Gif spelled backwards is "Fig?" Now that's clever thinking. Now go make friends with a patent attorney, and let's do this. It's never too late.

Chapter IV: Aging

*"Wrinkles mean you laughed,
gray hair means you cared,
and scars mean you loved."*

Memory Laps

I hate it when I gingerly climb up clad in my red patent stilettos set to perch on my SUV throne, and the seat is set in super-lumbargrandpa-position. The steering wheel is crushing my Body by Victoria boobs, my six-pack is thrust into the odometer and my peep toes don't even reach the floorboard. wtf? Mr. Wonderful drove my car again.

After I dislodge my delicate torso from the dashboard, I push the "go" button, and "My Way" crooned by my mother's under-thedaisies-heart-throb fills my tiny pink ears. How I hate that song (annoyingly appropriate for the circumstances). If I hear Frank's mellow voice once more, I swear I will leave Mr. Wonderful's Fruit of the Looms in the dryer on "Extra Shrink" over night.

"Seat Setting #1" is supposed to be high enough so I can see over the steering wheel with just enough space through the windshield so the purple-hairs and Crotch-Rocket creeps can see me flipping them off. The music is supposed to be turned back to **my** favorite channels: ZZ Tops High Tunes, Elvis Plugged and Naughty Girls Rock (Serious-ly)?

I check the gas gage, and, surprise, I have enough gas to get out of the garage. Is he kidding me? Just because he does the laundry, mops the floors, washes the cars, trims the hedges, cuts the lawn, grills the fish and scrubs the toilets, this does not give him permission to mess with my carriage. I have to get to the hair stylist's by 1:00, and I have just enough time to make it through the 87 lights. How am I going to find time to fill the tank too? This really sucks.

I pull into the station on fumes, and descend from my throne. Some wise guy at the next pump has the gall to say to me, "Hey, Blondie, nice ride." I take one look at his drool-laced beard and turn away. I put on my gold glove, thrust the nozzle into the gas tank and begin deep breathing. I can just feel him checking out my wheels. What? Do I hear "My Way" coming from the radio of his semi?

The Kids Don't Want It

Don't kid yourselves. Your kids don't want your stuff. Every time you buy a piece of furniture over $50 or a painting over $4000, think twice. The kids won't want it. They don't even want the family photos or the 8 millimeters. They want your cold cash and maybe your jewelry. If you have more than one child, they will all want the same thing.

Well, kids, guess what?

When we cleaned out my father's home of only 20 years, I had some hard decisions to make. Did we want the ball of string the size of a beach ball? He must have saved every piece since 1936. Did we want the mildew luggage from 1941? Did we want his collection of 3-way light bulbs that only worked two ways? (If we only knew which two). Did we want the 20 tiny daily journals in which my father kept a running account of the weather and his golf scores? Not really.

We did want all the letters he and my mother wrote to each other during World War II when my father was stationed in France and Belgium. Those are priceless.

I ask myself, "Which kids will want the sex toys? Which daughter will fight for the grand piano? Which one will say she has dibs on the sports car? Which one will want my collection of stilettos dating from 1962?" These are serious questions that could make you fart in the night.

You can fret about them, or you can just do what is necessary, and "let it rip, I mean let it go."

Simple Directions

To get to our house from downtown, just follow these simple directions. It shouldn't take more than 25 minutes allowing for traffic.

Start at the river and turn left. Look for the courthouse with the red tile roof and continue straight past the Shell gas station. Stay left, but turn right at the first Stop sign. Go about seven miles until you get to a green sign (above your head) that says Market Street. Go under the viaduct and turn right at the sign. If you end up at the ocean, you've gone too far. (Back up and go back to the sign).

Now this next part is tricky. Once you've turned at the sign, watch for the McDonald's on your left. Don't stop there. Continue past McDonald's about ten miles. You'll pass a sports bar, a used car dealership, a post office and a goat farm. Once you see the traffic light on your right, take a left.

Check in at the guard shack. Tell them you're coming to see us. If he doesn't know our name, you're in the wrong development. Go back and start over.

Update:

Now that you've got those directions down pat (who's "pat," anyway?), we've moved. It's hard to believe that anyone would ever give written or verbal directions anymore with the increased popularity of the GPS. This device is as crucial to my daily existence as Charmin Ultra Strong. I can't go anywhere without my GPS. It's the greatest invention since Pre-Nup.

The trick is to find our new home with it. Someone in the Cyber Test Drive Division didn't get the signals from Stanley Satellite. When you put in our address, it will get you within two blocks of our house, but then it wants to take you to George Fluckmuth's house on Paddington CV. We don't know George, and we still can't figure out what a CV is. You must stop at the Gate House, therefore, and tell the nice computer that the GPS is confused, and you need to find us. Hopefully, the computer will not be patched into the GPS system and will send you to us. Otherwise, we hope you and George enjoy the evening. Cheers!

The Great Recession

Who feels the Great Recession? Yours truly. It began when I was a kid when brushing your teeth harder meant better. It continued when I got braces, and they didn't do it right. It got worse as the years without flossing (no one knew about the advantages of flossing in my day) wreaked havoc on my pie hole. Now in the "golden years" (hah), the fragile foundation for my fangs is threatening to cause pain.

As with other parts of my anatomy that are feeling the effects of years of neglect and abuse, I am faced with the daunting task of "prevention." That old saying, "An ounce of prevention" is just hogwash. Why would anyone wash a hog anyway? He's just going to get all muddy again. That's like saying why brush your teeth? They're just going to get dirty again. They should have invented a gum prevention program years ago, and I wouldn't be in this conundrum.

At this tender age, I have determined that everything is in "limp" mode, including my finances. My "stash" of collagen, money and enzymes is on "almost empty." What's a girl to do? If you spend money to "refresh," it could backfire and everything will just disintegrate anyway, so you've spent the stash for nothing. If you don't spend it now, it could cause triple the expense later. So I ask myself, "Later? What's that in years and months? Two years? Ten years?" If I'm lucky, I'll only last another dozen, so what are the odds?

I've never been a gambler. Is this the time to start? Losing money when you're working is not good, but you can earn it back. Not so in retirement. If you lose your teeth when you're still in the mainstream, you can buy a set of implants and pay it back on the "Tough Luck" plan. Not so when you're on a "fixed" income. Someone neglected to "fix" mine, unfortunately, and that's why I'm in this mess.

Now I could just eat soft foods that don't get in between my molars for the rest of my life. That way, there would be no wear and tear on the foundation. I ask you, how many people have gum damage from cottage cheese or flan? Or, I could just take my chances, and hope I still have something left with which to chew a week from Thursday. Oh my. And you thought you had problems deciding whether to get Netflix or Amazon Prime.

At The Pearly Gates

I was thinking about having a party in Heaven. If I were to start planning now, I think by the time I'm ready, all questions will have been answered.

When planning a party in a venue one knows little about some questions arise:

1. Do they serve alcohol up there?
2. Do they wear clothes?
3. What are the floors like? Can you hire a band and dance?

    (or is there a DJ who only plays hymns?)
4. Can I wear my stilettos?
5. Is there a maximum number of guests allowed?
6. Can you say bad words?
7. Are there restrooms?
8. Is there a coat check?
9. Is there a curfew?
10. Is there a check-in procedure? name tags?

When I get there, will all the people who have gone there before me be waiting for me? Do I have to invite them to my party? Can my mother still boss me around and tell me to "zip it?"

Update:

We are six years closer to the Pearly Gates than our last view. This is not a good thing. We are really having a good time down here, and although I'm sure the real estate is cheap up there, and the spirits are kind, we really prefer the spirits down here, especially at Happy Hour.

It is no longer funny joking about the final move. We just emptied the last box from the "last move" the other day. The thought of packing everything up again to head due north isn't at all appealing. Cleaning up my language is going to take some time, and I still can't figure out what host gift to give the Big Gal. She probably has everything she needs by now with the gifts given by the multitudes of wealthy souls already settled there. Nope. Not ready yet. Thanks, but we don't even want to be on the wait list.

P.S. I know my dog, "Butch" is up there. Do I have to clean up after him?

The Mantra

I am really enjoying my new meditations. Today, the mantra was something like "abugatah." I said "abugatah" several times. Translation: "This is going to be a great day no matter how many times I try to fuck it up." Yup. These are sayings that are supposed to motivate us to keep our thoughts pure and our words sans venom.

Have you ever had days where everything that comes out of your pie hole is crap? I just want to take a tiny tweezers and pluck the syllables out of the air and stuff them back down my craw. What was I thinking? I know I will be posthumously humiliated, and any chance I might have had at sainthood will be squelched.

Then there are other days when the consonants resonate and the vowels are like velvet donuts escaping like little dough rings into the atmosphere. "Yes, Virginia. I do have days like that."

The mantra thing fascinates me though. Where do they come up with words that require three puckers per syllable? Why can't they just be happy with "mmmmmm?" This begs the question: Who is "they?" I assume they're monks from Nepal who haven't spoken for so many years, all they can get out are syllables. Words are superfluous. Now that I think about this, words have texture. For example, "pluck" is pithy, "flummoxed" is gritty, "harassed" is prickly, and "swan" is silky. Could you show me something in kumquat?

Hurry cane

During a recent hurricane, I was thinking about how one day, I might be hobbling around with a cane because the wooden box of love letters from my past 74 boyfriends had fallen on my head while I was cowering in the closet with my ear buds thrust into my ear canals. If you have never lived through 143 mile-an-hour winds, you've missed a real treat.

Waiting for a hurricane is like that feeling you get pausing at the top of the rollercoaster. You know it's a fast downward burst that could throw you out onto the cement 800 feet below, but you tell yourself, the survival odds are in your favor. Or not. You close your eyes, pray hard, grit your molars together hoping they won't crack, and you surrender to the terror.

Looking up at the bottom of my skirts from my closet floor, random thoughts race through my mind: Will I ever wear that cute flouncy number again? Will the rod break and my clothes suffocate me? Will the roof fly off and the rains drown me in booties? Will the floor buckle beneath me and suck me into China where children have no food? (That's what my Mom always told me when I wouldn't eat my spinach.) Why was I thinking about spinach when my life was careening past my pie hole?

I survived Irma, and hopefully, the alphabet will run out before I ever have to escape to the walk-in again, and, hopefully, by then, I will be walking in. If I ever have to use a cane, I will be sure to get several, each to match a specific pair of 4" booties.

Linked-in For Seniors

What is this thing called "Linked-In?" When they invented this concept, Mr. Wonderful and I had already retired. We didn't need jobs, although twelve years later, it would be awesome to have the income.

This is my understanding of the way it operates. You create a "Profile" and put the very best photo of yourself on there. The "Profile" includes every good thing you've ever done for anyone you've ever worked for. For example, if you bumped into your colleague's brand new Beamer in the parking lot and left a corn-on-the-cob-sized dent, you confessed tearfully and offered to pay for it. This would be considered a "good thing." Or if someone in your department came up with a really fabulous way to reach the bottom line, and you didn't take credit for it, which would also be considered "a good thing." You can even ask your colleagues to write testimonials. The Linked-In robot sends them out to everyone you know.

Other items to include on your Profile are awards you've earned along the way. For example, I was voted "Most likely to write a feckless blog for four years." Such accomplishments can take you far when you're looking for a new career. Or not.

The Profile Picture is crucial, as people can judge you by your appearance before they even read your Profile. The vintage of the photo seems to be random. People post their high school graduation photos, their first divorce photos, their early death photos—no matter. Professional photos can make you look twenty years younger. The problem is that you aren't.

Once you are all signed up, you "Link" with others who have also found the "Kodak Moment." You will then receive a message from the Linked-In robot that tells you that you have a new "Linked-In" connection. It doesn't matter if you haven't seen or heard from this person since 1951.

The real motivator is the automated message that says, "Three people have read your Profile." When you try to find out who is stalking you, the message reads, "In order to find out who is looking for you, you must sign up for the next level of communication. This is only $86.32 per month." Click here." What?

Sex After Seventy

Terminology For Retirees

1. Huh?
2. Where did I put. . .
3. I did not.
4. Who cares?
5. I don't get it.
6. I could have told them that.
7. Why would they even go there?
8. What is this world coming to?
9. Where are the parents?
10. If they'd just put down their damned phones. . .
11. Why am I so tired all the time?
12. How long are you going to let those things sit there? It's been a year and a half.
13. Are you effen kidding me?
14. Where's a 10-year-old when I need her?
15. In my day. . .
16. There's no ——— anymore.
17. When I get around to it.
18. I'm out of Raisin Bran.
19. I don't feel like it.
20. You never told me that.

Legacy

Have you ever thought about what legacy you will leave? These thoughts only begin to surface when you pass your 50th birthday. All of you under 50 can turn to the recipe section. Good luck with that.

What do you do, say, wear, model that will go down in your family's history? Who will thank you for something when you're gone? What will they say about you? Whose lives have you touched? What would you have done differently?

Those questions don't belong in this book; they would be better off discussed with your therapist.

I will leave behind my liver spots, my bulging-vein hands, my adorable little-girl nose, my double-jointed thumbs and my performance addiction. How about you?

And what about secrets. Will you let the world discover yours after you're gone? Did you leave a diary, an attempt at your memoirs, a letter, a true confession, a velvet zippered change purse with your secret stash neatly folded? (See Dear Diary, Memoirs, "The Let-ter.")

Best Movies and Books For Seniors

1. Citizen Cane
2. From Chair to Eternity
3. Home Sweet Home
4. Dirty Fancying
5. Taken
6. Grapes in Bath
7. Dream Lover
8. Broken
9. Full Moon and Empty Charms
10. It's All about the Face

Chapter V:
Words and Writing

---

*"The dubious privilege of a
freelance writer is he's given the
freedom to starve anywhere."*

S.J. Perlman

Voice Over

I always wanted to do a voiceover. Now my voice is over. Yup. No more voice. Years ago, I sang in prestigious choral groups, and I even had my own trio for a while. At that time, I had a resonant alto voice, and I could harmonize to anything or next to anyone. Those were the days, my friends. No longer. I open my pie hole, and not a single note comes out. Occasionally, a tiny squeak will emerge, but it never lasts longer than a nanosecond. Why does anyone care? No one does. They say it's a muscle, and if you practice diligently, you can get it back. Maybe there's a Viagra for the vocal chords?

Death By Syllables

"STOP TALKING!" came out of my 14-year-old grandson's mouth numerous times in the three short days we were visiting. His cry was always directed at his eight-year-old brother who has a gift for gab (talks non-stop). I found that during this visit the young funny man was rather quiet in comparison to other visits, but maybe it's because I don't live in their world, as the 12-year-old brother suggested. The amusing part of this story is that there are so many times every week that I want to scream these words to someone—not children—adults, sometimes even friends who just don't know when to quit. As the Emperor, Joseph II, said to Mozart—"too many notes," I want to scream "TOO MANY WORDS. ENOUGH!"

There are certain people who have no clue how much they talk. I am forced to listen because I am way too polite, I have discovered warning signs disguised in the following:

"because. . . "
"Let me tell you a story."
"And then, you won't believe what happened . . ."
"I'll make this short."
"I won't bore you with the details."
"We started the first day of our six-week trip by. . . "
"To get there, you start by. . . "
"The ingredients are somewhat unusual."
"My opinion on this very controversial issue is . . ."

Oh, Lord, please spare me. Anytime I hear any of the above, I know I'm screwed. This monologue could last anywhere from ten minutes to thirty, and my cheeks can only shift 13 times per paragraph.

What's wrong with people? Do they not know this is the 21st century, and troubadours are out? Did anyone tell them about taking a breath or watching for the "glazed look?" No matter what body language I give these people from looking at the ceiling to rolling my eyes to standing up and sighing loudly, they just keep talking. "Stop Talking!"

If I'm lucky, the people flapping their jaws are mildly interesting, and if God is looking down on me, they're even funny. Funny is fabulous; interesting is good. Boring is death by syllables.

This begs the question: Who is more guilty of dominating a conversation? Men or women? As a female, I hate to say it, but we are guilty not so much of dominating, but of detailing. Some of us feel that every color, fabric, molecule, ingredient, attitude must be explained. They do not. No one cares. As a male friend once said to me, "Cut to the chase." Another kinder male, said, "Ba dip ba dip ba dip." I got the message. (Fortunately for Mr. Wonderful, that was in 1974)

Men, au contraire, dominate. Some just talk over anyone who has a tiny little opinion or wants to utter an "uh huh." Polite idiots like me just smile and listen, gritting our molars.

When I grow up, I want to be rude.

TYVM

I've never been able to figure out why, when someone runs into me, I am the one to apologize. I am just standing there minding my own business, and some moron practically knocks me over. Instead of the moron apologizing to me, I jump right in and say, "Oh, excuse me." What? Why am I the one apologizing? It's an automatic polite reflex originating from my FOO (Family of Origin). The killer is the response I always hear, "Oh, you're fine." Wtf. I'm fine? "No, I'm not fine, idiot. You almost knocked me over."

In the old days, we were taught to say, "Excuse me" when we were at fault. The real old people said, "I beg your pardon." That must have come from the French expression, "Je vous en prie," which literally translates, "I beg it of you." That expression now means, "You're welcome." What?

Well, when you run into me, do not tell me I am fine. I'm not. Worse than that, some people even say, "No worries." I have worries, so don't tell me not to, and one of my worries is running into morons like you, tyvm.

*thankyouverymuch."

Too Many Words

The king said of Mozart's music, "Too many notes." He was right about that, and I know that firsthand because years ago I tried playing Mozart's piano music. No way. Way too many notes.

There are also too many words—words that have multiple meanings, and this can be confusing to any woman over 65 and any man over 30. Here are some examples:

1. circulation -
    What library books do.
    What old people have to think about.
    What the French know as "traffic."

2. unhinged
    Off the hinge
    Behavior of certain politicians who tweet in the dark.

3. spam
    Things sent to your mailbox that you don't want.
    Meat from the 50s.

4. paradigm
    a concept embraced by a certain number of people
    $.20

5. fake news
    Anything coming out of Washington.

6. Consensus
    No longer in common use

7. coma
    people who can't spell comma

8. gif
    something you give to a friend for a birthday
    fig spelled backwards

9. emoji
    images for people who have no vocabulary

10. best seller
    What the ignorant masses read

11. overwhelm
    opposite of underwhelm (What is a "whelm" anyway?)

12. app
    first syllable of a group of words (application,
    appointment, apparently)
    what parents try to hide from their kids

13. rap
    What used to be nonsense language of 3rd graders
    Some version of music with a weird message
    Something old people wear

14. screen
    a way to see if people are sane
    something to keep insects out
    a way to discriminate
    where everyone's face is from 7 a.m. to 11 p.m.

15. hang
    a way to attach a picture
    a manner of putting clothes on a line
    sitting one's ass somewhere for an extended period

Chapter VI: WTF?

*"After MONDAY and TUESDAY,
even the calendar says, WTF."*

Kale

I am absolutely convinced there is someone out there trying to force the worst tasting plants in the universe into my pie hole. Who came up with this one? Kale? Are you kidding me? Kale is just wrong. It's way too green to be real. Someone has certainly put food coloring into it to get it to be such a perfect Crayola "Tropical Rain Forest Green." The texture is for someone with bionic incisors. If you chew it too long, the insides of your cheeks will be shredded. And then there's the taste. It's a combination of week-old spinach and pickled cardboard. No one should eat this no matter how healthy it is. I suggest that if you purchase this crap, you should put some aside to use as a scrub brush or a foot exfoliator.

What Day Is It?

Did you ever think it was Saturday, and it was really Thursday? All day long, you're walking around in Saturday. You go to your closet to get ready to go out, and you realize it's Thursday. Then when Saturday shows up, you feel like you've already done this day. But you haven't because it was Thursday when you thought it was Saturday. So now you're not sure if tomorrow is Friday or Sunday. You are afraid to show up at church just in case it's Friday, so you don't go. Then, however, you start feeling guilty, and based on the lack of traffic, you're now convinced it's not Friday; it must be Sunday, and you didn't say your Sunday prayers. You feel ashamed. You think this feels painful like Monday. You know it's not Monday though because the alarm didn't go off. Sometimes, the alarm doesn't work though, so now you're questioning clocks as well as calendars. Suddenly, you stop dead. You shake yourself, and say, "Wtf day is it? I think it's Tuesday." And off you go to the library to pay your fine. Except the sign on the library door says, "Closed for the Holiday." You don't know if the holiday was Monday or Wednesday, so you dig your cell out of the cup holder where it's been charging for a week. Seri is yelling, "You moron. If you have a question, just ask me. Do you even know what day it is?"

Men's Junk

Men's junk comes in all sizes and shapes. It can be found in drawers, pockets, toolboxes, and in packages of various dimensions.

Men love to play with their junk. I have never quite understood this, but I have observed this playfulness for years. They always get a charge out of the experience no matter how long it is.

Men are also obsessed with their junk. They think about it regularly. Women don't even have to be present for them to be focused on packages of it or drawers full of it.

When they are asked to clean out their junk, men frown, and some even whine. They might take out their junk, but that's as far as it goes. Many have trouble arranging it, and they use this as an excuse to continue their obsession.

One would think that it was some kind of family jewel.

"Happy" Rejection

So I'm watching 60 Minutes, and there are a handful of cartoonists sitting around the table at the New Yorker magazine waiting for their cartoons to be accepted for publication. The main guy takes a cursory look at each one, rejects most and chooses an occasional submission. The artists sit waiting to be rejected. I am thinking, "Are you effen kidding me? You have to sit there and be humiliated in front of each other while one person decides your fate?" And these people do this for a living?

A few minutes later, they interview the artists alone. One guy says, "I'm addicted to rejection. It makes me feel alive." What??! I can honestly say I have never looked at rejection from this angle. Being a person who tries to have an open mind about things, I say to myself, "Ok, self. Just think, if no one rejects you, you're dead."

The artists said that out of 700-800 cartoons they submit each year, they get about 30 published. Oh, my. I hope they don't play the stock market.

In my new book, The Four Agreements, which I have read at least five times, one of the agreements is to never take anything personally. How could you not take that rejection personally? The theory is that anyone who hurts, insults, criticizes you is talking about himself, not you. So if you know that, you will never be offended, and therefore you and what's-his-hat can just sing "HAPPY" the rest of your days. Yeah, right.

More Recipes From My Mom

My Inner Bitch

Every so often, my inner bitch ratchets up and puts on a show all her own. This is the "one-woman show" I don't rehearse. It's as Dan Harris describes in his book, the "malevolent puppeteer" gone mad. Yes, the strings are attached, and they are creating a bitch ballet of unimaginable proportion. Anyone who dares enter the stage during this tantrum is risking serious injury.

We all have inner voices, but the one that takes center stage is our own voice that narrates every action we take and every thought we choose or don't choose to act upon. (Grammarians, "Bite me!") Yes, that voice begins the minute I wake up in the morning, and it follows me to bed every night, sometimes even waking me up to tell me what a bitch I am.

My inner bitch sometimes discovers other voices that have snuck in when she was busy ranting or thank-the-Lord napping. These voices always appear uninvited, and they can wreak havoc if Ms. Bitch is in one of her moods. I hear her arguing with them. "What the hell are you doing here? I thought you died. wtf." There's "I told you so," "What are you thinking?" "You'd better not do that," and "You will fail." Sometimes the voices have ugly faces; other times, they are faceless with messages that sound like a recording played at a way-too-slow speed so they sound like monsters in a tunnel. The conversations that take place usually produce migraines or wine-bottle time-outs.

What does your inner bitch say? Does she come and go, or is she there all the time? I have determined that hormones seem to throw her off balance, and wine tends to make her more surly, but, thankfully, occasionally mellow.

"What?" All right. I know. I've got this. You didn't have to remind me. Jeez.

Poem

There once was a woman named Alice
She wanted to live in a palace
She was young and quite fair
she had lots of hair
but her fate took her straight to south Dallas.

Her eyes were so sparkly and bright
so lovely she looked late at night
but time took its toll
her beauty it stole
and now sweet Alice is a fright.

Crows feet stick out from her eyes
cellulite threatens her thighs
her face has huge jowls
which give way to scowls
Poor Alice just mutters and cries.

Her hair began thinning, alas
her arms got all crepey, poor lass
her teeth turned to yellow
no longer was she mellow
and soon disappeared her sweet ass.

Politics

Anyone who dares to bring up politics in a public place is risking confrontation, condemnation and possibly flogging with a tech device. Politics is off the table. With the divisiveness in our country, even your preacher can't save you, and she probably has her own opinions, based on Leviticus 42:3-59.

The terms Republican and Democrat elicit such ire that you're better off admitting to being a kale-freak than to admit your political preference.

Common arguments such as boxers versus briefs, kale versus romaine, prunes versus flaxseed, pro versus con, mauve versus magenta, it's all so overwhelming, yet much safer than which congress person harassed Miss Piggy.

In the good old days, you could talk about such simple subjects as "Weapons of Mass Destruction," the Crash," Sonoma versus Napa," "foam versus feather," and never have a problem. People discussed these topics with dignity and grace. No longer. Ever since "Kalegate," it's been all downhill.

Just think about it. Who would even want to be President of this country? You're setting yourself up for so much criticism and scrutiny. People want to know what you tweet before bed, for heavens sake. A woman President? The world would be dying to know how many layers of Retinae you use before bed, how many times you get up to pee, and why your eye shadow only sparkles on your left eyelid. Ah, that's the one you wink with. I get it.

Chapter VII: Archives

Got The Toc,
Where's The Tic?

I just mailed a chunk of my ego to 14 publishers. Somewhere between New York City and Portland, Oregon, my little query letter sits on someone's desk waiting to be read.

A preoccupied publishing executive will meander into his office, coffee cup in hand and sit down in front of a pile of envelopes like mine eagerly waiting to be given their two minutes of scrutiny. How is mine different than everyone else's? Who knows? The main difference is that my ego exudes from the rhetoric.

Does this person have any clue how many hours, how much sweat and angst went into the book I'm trying to pitch? He or she obviously does not care. There has to be a trick to getting my query noticed, but I'm at a loss to know what it might be. When I get my rejection letter, I will know that whatever it was—I didn't have it.

I have read many books about authors who failed, authors who received hundreds of rejections before being published. Some of them even lived long enough to see the first run of their book printed. I don't have a lot of time, as I'm approaching the "golden" years. (Good news, gold is up) Hopefully, it will only take me a couple hundred of such "sorry"s before the magic letter comes that says,

"This is a phenomenal concept! Send us the toc and sample chapters immediately." Ok, maybe I'm dreaming, but miracles happen, and I have an indomitable spirit.

I would send a photo of my really sexy legs if I thought that would help, but my sources say that's tacky. I could tell them that my house is in foreclosure and that my husband will leave me if I don't get published, but that would only be partially true. I could send a photo of my daughter in her bikini saying it was me, and wouldn't I look great in the press releases, but that would be cheating. Besides, my daughter wears a one-piece (one never knows which one).

No, I must hope that the integrity of my writing will knock out the publisher, and he or she will be hooked after the first paragraph.

According to my research, only 16% of writers can earn a living writing. I don't let that daunting figure stop me. I boldly lick the envelopes, spend my life savings on SASEs and run to the mailbox daily to retrieve my sentence. Once I've accumulated at least 50 to 100 rejection letters, I will know it's time to start getting ready for the big times. Oprah, here I come. Oops, she left.

Un-Glib

Today I am "out of sorts." What is a sort anyway? Can you be in sorts? When was the last time someone walked up to you and said, "Wow, you look like you are totally in sorts today." Sorts shmorts. I am out of them.

Yesterday, I had "time on my hands." Why would you only have time on your hands? Where is the time? In between your fingers? crawling up your lifeline? on the balls of your thumbs? Why don't we have time on our knees or time on our ribs? If we had time on our hands too often, it would put the watchmakers out of business. How sad would that be?

"It's on the tip of my tongue," my friend said. So, why doesn't she just reach in there, scrape it off and come out with it. Why would it go from wherever it was, rush to the tip of her tongue and simply stop? That's absurd. Besides, we don't vocalize from our tongues, do we? Isn't the larynx involved?

"At the end of the day," has become one of the most over-used expressions of the twenty-first century. If someone says that again, I swear I am going to send them a Weiner gram. First of all, when does the day end? Is it midnight? Is it when you go to bed? Is it when it starts to get dark? These six words are meaningless. Maybe backwards would be more catchy, "Day the of, end the at." Hmm. Now that has a certain cadence, n'est-ce pas?

"Without further ado. . ." What's an ado? Who says "ado" without a "without further?" An "ado" is a bustle. I rather like "without further bustle." It has a certain joviality and actually sounds quite British, would you say?

"Ya know?" No, I don't. If I knew, you would not have to ask now, would you?

"I rest my case." Where do I rest it though? And what kind of a case might it be? A suitcase? A briefcase? A mental case? A basket case? And how can a person actually "rest" something. When you put something down, it rests itself. The person cannot make it rest. It's out of the person's control. At the end of the day, it's no wonder I'm out of sorts. Maybe I have too much time on my hands.

"Go figure." What figure are we talking about? If its mine, I certainly don't want to "go" there. And where am I supposed to "go?"

Whenever I say, "I'm sorry" or "Excuse me," the response is usually "No worries." People used to say, "That's all right". Now it's "No worries." I find this expression quite comforting. If I really had "no worries," that would certainly be "all right."

Update:

Here we are four years later, and people are still filling the air with these feckless figures of speech. Not to be outdone, there are more. Wait. What's "outdone?" Is there an "indone?" And what on earth does that mean? If you're done, you're done, so who cares if it's in or out?

There's this new word, "meme." This one really annoys me. My nickname for grandma is "Mémé." That's "meme" with appropriate French accents to accurately describe an old woman who has little kids hanging from her knees. Every time, someone writes "meme," I'm thinking they're talking to me. "Même" with the circumflex accent in French means "same." None of these are the same, so this just confounds the issue further.

"Texting" is not only a new word; it represents a generation of mutes. Yes, "text" which used to mean a book that students used to read and learn has now become a cult word for typing something quickly on a cell phone with no effort to spell or punctuate. A simple example would be, "I no u will b ther." This means the person is coming. That is totally absurd to write on a phone anyway. "Texting" is a noun, and the verb "text" means to code as described above. Once they took cursive out of the schools, I knew it was all downhill.

"Twitter" used to be the lovely sound of a bird. It used to represent delight and joy. No longer. "Twitter" is how people confront. They type in the middle of the night, sending outrageous messages to piss people off. This does not go along with any bird thoughts other than flipping them. I have often used the word "twit," for people who act like idiots, but a "twit" is not necessarily a "twitter" (one who twits), and the whole thing makes me crazy.

Then there's "Fomo" and "Jomo." "Fomo" means "fear of missing out," and "Jomo" means "Joy of missing out." There's a message here. Some people are just not up to more than a syllable or a half phrase. Let me get this straight: Complete sentences are out, and grammar is v archaic. Not only are people not willing to talk in syllables; they are too lazy to write them too. This whole new vocab is putting me in a twit. Lord help us.

How Clean Is My Cuisine?

I have this friend who doesn't cook. When we visited her lovely home for cocktails before going out for dinner, she proudly showed me her cooktop that she said she has never used. "Never used?" I gasped. "You don't cook at all?" "Not really," she replied. "We either go out or order something to bring back in for dinner. I stopped cooking when we retired and moved here five years ago." I could not believe my ears. Was this awesome, or what? I had never heard of someone who not only did not cook but was actually proud of it.

After returning home, I contemplated this concept. Not being the world's greatest chef, but wishing I were, I asked myself what advantage there would be to not cooking dinner every night, other than the obvious not having to clean up. My friend doesn't cook for guests either, obviously, so entertaining is simply cheese and crackers and a glass of wine before heading to the restaurant of choice.

Entertaining is something I thoroughly enjoy now that my husband and I can be in the kitchen together without killing each other (this took about 13 years of our 18 together). Looking at the recipes from the last dinner party (for six), I decided to do a financial analysis of the ingredients, the bottles of wine, the fresh flowers, the new dripless candles and the latest elegant classical disc. The entrée called for at least four ingredients that I had never heard of nor will

I ever use again: walnut oil, Rose Hip something or other, crème fraîche and enoki. The bottle of walnut oil was $6.95. I needed one teaspoon. The Rose Hip thingy was $3.95, the crème fraîche was $5.95 and the enoki was $9.95. This came to almost $30.00 of which I needed about $1.72 worth. Hmmmm. Then I had to purchase enough wine for my wino friends—at least three bottles. I couldn't bring myself to buy my usual Two Buck Chuck version, so I spent $50 on the wine, of which I drank about three ounces, my husband, none.

The entrée was beef tenderloin, which I got at a bargain price of $22.95 per pound. The beef totaled close to $70.00. I had two ounces; my husband had about 4.3 ounces. The vegetable course, roasted root veggies, ran about $18, and the fingerling potatoes were about $11.00.

I chose a simple dessert, a fresh fruit trifle. The fruit alone was $16.00. My grand total sans hors d'oeuvres came to close to $200. I am counting nothing for the three days I spent cleaning the house, the gas to go to four stores to buy the necessary supplies and the angst worrying about whether it was all going to taste good and be piping hot. We could have gone to the best restaurant in town and had a super gourmet feast for under $120. Hmmmm.

The flowers lasted all of two days, and the disc got a scratch on it the first time we played it. The good news is, however, that our guests raved about the meal and stayed until 2:00 a.m. finishing up the final drops of Conundrum.

After analyzing my three-day bank and backbreaking routine, I have decided that having a flawless, pristine cook top has genuine merit. Now if I can just find some very cheap cheese and get me some Bogo Triscuits, life will be good.

Update: 2017

In our new home, I am proud to say that my cooktop is clean. It is clean because I've used it many times, and Mr. Wonderful has cleaned it regularly. Other things have changed, however.

First of all, we have regressed in our entertaining efforts. Because I am so fanatic about having the house perfectly neat and clean, and because I want the meal to be elegant and savory, I tend to get a bit tense. He does not like tense, even though "Tense" is his middle name. We had some "words" before our last dinner party, and as a result, we haven't entertained since. I've asked myself, "Is it time to stop entertaining, and just offer the nice wine and Triscuits?" It sure would take pressure off. People could enjoy the comfort of our new home, perhaps even listen to me tickle the ivories, and off we can go to the nearest award-winning restaurant. We aren't sure about this yet, but neither of us is willing to have "the conversation" about preparation for company. One easy solution would be to hire a cleaning person so I could focus on the cooking. (I hate cooking, so why do I want to focus on it?) Of course, it would be my responsibility to pay the cleaning person. This does put a different spin on things.

Secondly, there is the expense of the meal as outlined in 2013. Add inflation, budget adjustments and motivation. These all beg the question of whether I even want to have "the conversation."

Finally, by inviting people to dinner, they will get the false impression that we actually enjoy all this work and expense, and that is downright hypocritical.

You guessed it. No conversation. No words. No entertaining. Just looking for Triscuit coupons.

How About A Joint?

The last time I had a "joint" checking account was 1967. Hubby #1 had no idea when he agreed to this plan how our checkbook register would appear. He just had his nice healthy paycheck deposited into the account and let me go. After a couple of months, he began questioning my entries. "What's 'P. U. K.' on February 12?" "Oh, that's Pick Up Kids," I chirped. "And what's '7101916' on February 2nd?" "That's my Dad's birthday. I need to be thinking about his gift." "His birthday is in July," he said. "You can never plan too far ahead," I say.

These dialogues were friendly at first, but midway through the year, Hubby #1 began showing signs of needing a joint to deal with the joint. "You used four lines in the check register to list the dog's vet appointments for the next three years? That is not a transaction description." "Of course it is. When I take the dog to the vet, there is always a transaction," I countered. I explained to him my understanding of the terms in the register.

The first column "number or code" was where I indicated the nature of the purchase. For example, "tam" stood for "Tint and Manicure." "Gim" represented "Groceries Including Meat." "Sfm" was "Something For moi ." The Transaction Description had more than enough room to write the receiver of the check plus my abbreviated daily "to do" list. "Deposit check" was totally superfluous, as our checks automatically deposited, so that space is always available for me to practice my cartooning. The box with the dollar sign on it (apparently for the balance) is the amount of *my money* left to spend. I liked to keep track in our checkbook of the amount of discretionary income that was reserved just for me. Usually I included $50 or so from the grocery budget, as I knew some hefty coupons would soon show up in the mail.

My unique system of monitoring our money was beginning to work on Hubby #1. His blood pressure was climbing, and his patience was running thin. Finally, when he could no longer stand trying to decipher my domestic drivel, he suggested we get individual checking accounts. Having recently read an article about how to be an independent spouse, I agreed, and the bleeding stopped.

Update:

Who has a checking account in the 21st century? Yup, Mr. Wonderful. I have recently helped him set up paying his bills on "Bill Pay" through our bank. What a concept. He's thrilled, and now he only has to write 46 checks per month.

I love it when you write a check to an organization, and they keep it until all the other members send theirs in. This usually takes a minimum of six to seven weeks. In the meantime, as I only write this one check per month, I forget about it, and have almost gotten overdrawn. The Treasurer, the nice white-haired lady who used to be treasurer of her Girl Scout troop, hasn't gotten around to cashing the checks yet. If you are stupid enough to get overdrawn in the 21st century, they will fine you quadruple the amount you paid down on your mortgage and take it out of your "He-has-no-idea-stash" account. This is very annoying, not to mention hard to explain when they send the overdrawn notice to him, not you. It is at this point that I must pull out the "Remember, I pay for your groceries" card. Life is so complicated at times.

Voices In My Head

The "Right Thing" Voice

The "RT" voice really sucks. Every time I want to buy something for myself, this voice reminds me of all the starving people in Wenogotstuffstan who don't even have a currency. It further brings to mind all of those envelopes in my "Current Annoyances" folder that beg me for money by sending me 974 address labels with my name spelled incorrectly. I just want to buy a damned blouse; I don't need a conscience cleansing.

The "Should" Voice

This voice should be shot, cremated and forgotten. This voice keeps me from saying nasty things about extremely hateful people; it prevents me from savoring that extra bite of to-die-for cheesecake; it forces me to do the "RT," and we already know that sucks.

The "What's Wrong With You" Voice

This voice took over with the passing of all relatives with common sense and conscience.

It's the "You Know Better," "Didn't We Teach You Anything," "You Ought to be Ashamed of Yourself," "God Will Punish You" voice. Some days, this voice can just keep you hidden under the down.

The "I Look Better Than That" Voice

This voice is extremely dangerous. It fools us into thinking that there is some imaginary scale (crafted by our own egos) that puts us a notch above the rest of the world. The instant cure for this one is a quick look in the mirror.

The "I Might Get Caught" Voice

If there is any chance of doing something wrong and getting caught, I will. If I speed up to try to make the light, I will receive a photo of my back bumper in the mail with a $50 charge. If I tailgate the bitch ahead of me after she cut me off, I will stall the car, and someone will plow into me. If I sneak a few dollars out of the grocery fund for my new blouse, I will get to the store and find that they have only sold the ones in my size.

Running For Office

I don't need a petition to be a candidate because I qualify by being a married woman with children. All married women qualify. I don't have to file, show proof of passing the bar or declare residency. I qualify because I am human and female. This office holds no responsibility, just freedom and peace. It is located on the second floor of our house, and I can lock myself in there anytime I feel harassed, unappreciated, overwhelmed or crazy. I love my office; it is my refuge. I don't have to clean it or decorate it. All I have to do is run for it. All parties know that my presence in this office means KEEP OUT.

To be honest, sometimes I do not pass the bar (the fully-stocked portable one) on the way up. I might even bring a bottle with me, but that's only in times of extreme hormones. Normally, I just take the steps two at a time and exhale at the top.

There are specific omissions in this place: mirrors, makeup, curling irons, bills, sharp instruments, to do lists, drugs, phones. This office is all about me. It is equipped with teddy bears, my *Pretty Woman* DVD, cuddly throws, travel brochures, framed diplomas, trophies, green plants, fresh flowers, and framed glamour shots from 1974.

There are no term limits to this office. I make policy when meditating or assuming the cobra pose and have been known to stay in session here for days at a time, surviving on ego alone. No one can vote me out, unseat me or impeach me. I am in total control here, and there is only one mood: good.

Husbands and children benefit by the lack of a mother. They grow up, man-up and show up.

Who knew?

Note From The Author:

I sincerely hope you have enjoyed an essay or twelve. We all think about many of these topics, but there are few feckless females who try to articulate these profound braindrips for the benefit of the gender.

Most of these jewels have been crafted before 5:30 a.m. It is then that solitude, caffeine and crazy congeal and banal is born.

When I was thirteen years old, a family friend and Editor of our local newspaper read a poem I wrote that won a prize. He labeled it "Doggerel." Well, I proved to him that he was barking up the wrong tree, didn't I?

Never let a man hold you back from your calling. Do not let him shame you into literary submission. There is always wisdom in the female pen, and this one's ink is overflowing.

"Fifi, la folle," 2018.

The following pages, written two years later, offer fun and chuckles and even a fresh Chalkduster font. Enjoy!

Corona Conundrum

Day #47 of "Shelter in Place"

Dear Diary:

This really sucks. My day begins in the dark, as I can't sleep worrying about how I am going to get through another day "sweltering in place." Yes, I said, "sweltering," not "sheltering," because we live in Florida, and NEWSBREAK: It's effen hot here.

I'd like to tell you that I'm losing weight from sweating so much, but that would be a lie. You see, we have now set aside "shelter snack time" by the pool. Yup. We consume at least a pound of Salmon Dip on Triscuits every afternoon, taking a pool dip in between courses. No, we don't swim it off in the pool. We just stand there and let the water feature massage the flab. It's an amazing rush.

When we aren't snacking, we're having protein after our workouts. Yes, we do workout. I am up to about eight minutes per day now, and I read that every workout should be followed by a portion of protein. Of course, no one said how much protein you should consume, so I have limited mine to two cups of ice cream with chocolate sauce. No worries, it's dark chocolate, and that's supposed to be good for my coat. Because we are in the "high-risk" population, we aren't allowed to go anywhere that "normal" people go. If we get too much fresh air, they fear we will become asymptomatic, and then we will spread it to other old farts like us. Notice the "normal" people. They are the ones carrying rifles and axes to the state capitals to protest being denied their rights. What about us? Don't we have a constitutional right to be "asymptomatic?"

Despite the fact that Mr. Wonderful only sleeps through the night once every six days, he does take numerous short naps to catch up. That would be fine, but I must be quiet during those times. I can't practice my piano, turn on the TV, listen to the radio, make a phone call or do my workout on the computer. What about wives' constitutional rights? Those are called "boundaries," and I forgot to set them 26 years ago. I know, I'm stupid.

Do you remember when your baby didn't sleep through the night? What did you do? You drugged the kid, right? Well, try drugging an 80-year-old. He can't see the pill much less swallow it. And you don't want to hear about the side effects, especially over breakfast.

How do I apply for a sabbatical? Do they still give those? During a global pandemic? Is there a salary? I need to be "dis-placed." This "shelter" shit sucks.

Corona Closet: Wardrobe Texts

Several items in my closet have been private messaging and texting me. I must admit, I haven't thought much about clothes since the Pandemic began. Like most of my friends, I wear the same three pairs of shorts and tank tops all week, just laundering them to save face. No one sees me, so there is no urgency to dress in "normal" threads in "surreal" times.

Here are a few of the recent messages I've received:

Favorite Stilettos: "Hey, girlfriend, I've been cooped up in this friggin' closet for way too long. Are you still alive?"

Dressy Sandals: "So have you become a recluse, or when am I going to meet the new cocktail dress you told me you were going to wear for New Years?"

Brand new designer dress: "Hello? Hello? Are you still breathing? It's lonely in here, and I really want to feel your arms in mine. How long do you intend to keep me in hiding?"

Cute Denim flouncy dress: "You were in such a hurry to buy me. Was that just a joke, or are you ever planning to let me feel your skin next to my zipper?"

Performance gown: "Have you gone into retirement? wtf. I am going limp hanging here with no applause."

Designer purse: "Are you broke? I've been feeling empty for months now. Have you moved on to a wallet? At least identify the competition."

Jean Jacket: "I suppose you don't think it's cool to wear denim anymore. Are you too old? Just pair me with a pair of stilettos and some skinny jeans, and we can stun those youngsters, girlfriend."

Coat: "Do I have to wait until you move north to wrap my arms around you? Will that happen in the 21st century? Please advise."

Songs to Survive a Pandemic

1. DON'T FENCE ME IN
2. NINETY-NINE BOTTLES OF BEER ON THE WALL
3. SIGNS
4. SHOW ME THE WAY TO LEAVE HOME
5. NOBODY KNOWS THE TROUBLES I'VE SEEN
6. TOO CLOSE FOR COMFORT
7. CRAZY
8. LET IT BE
9. I'VE GROWN ACCUSTOMED TO YOUR FACE
10. WAKE ME UP WHEN SEPTEMBER ENDS

Quarantine Classifieds 2020

Wanted: TP, toweling, sanitary wipes, Vodka

URGENT: Desperately seeking punching bag and weed

FAKE NEWS: We are all just fine.

HELP WANTED: Congress with common sense

JOB OPPORTUNITY: Mother to teen-agers

WANTED: New home for kale

SEEKING: Man to embrace my inner hubba

BALD WOMEN: Blonde frizz looking for new home

FOR SALE: Modest home, family included

Pandemic Pantry

MIDDLE SHELF (easiest to access)
1. Vodka
2. Scoops
3. Cookies
4. Wine

Bottom Shelf (when middle shelf is empty)
1. Vodka
2. Peanut butter
3. Chocolate bars
4. Tums

TOP SHELF (when Pandemic comes to an end)
1. Champagne
2. Vodka
3. Kleenex
4. Whisky
5. Cosmo mix
6. More vodka

Topics for Zoom Calls

1. What you've learned about him after nine days of confinement

2. How many faces you've found in the bathroom tile

3. What's happening in the latest episode of West Wing

4. What new takeout place you found

5. Who do you know who's got it?

6. How many times can you hear him say that and not lose your mind?

7. How wonderful life was "bTL" (before the lockdown)

8. How you don't trust any of your friends.

9. How to do third grade math

10. How do you punish an adult?

11. What bitch you encountered at the grocery store at 7:10 a.m.

12. How many books you read today

13. What color your hair is becoming

14. Creative uses for an exercise ball

15. How badly do you need razor blades?

16. The wisdom of tongue biting

17. How you miss people you hate

18. Who's running this show?

19. What ifs?

20. How many times you've gotten dressed this week

Surviving 90 Days Of Confinement

Equipment:

1. Netflix, Hulu, Amazon Prime, Acorn, Vodka

2. Headphones, nose plugs, egg shell slippers, duct tape

3. Car keys, cold cash, Amazon gift card stash, affectionate feline

4. Zoom, Face Time, personal computer, free weights, therapist

5. Punching bag, large pillows, rope, Pinot Grigio.

6. Audible, convertible, Red Bull, Xanax

7. Sense of humor, nerves of steel, positive attitude, Crown Royal

Aging: Not Going There!

Senior Workout

1. Wake up.

2. Get chair.

3. Rest.

4. Think about why you got chair.

5. Put chair in front of mirror.

6. Stop crying.

7. Rest.

8. Turn on music. (Recommended choices: "Let It Be," "Don't Get Around Much Anymore," "Signs," "All of Me.")

9. Tap foot to music.

10. Rest.

11. Sit in chair with legs together and feet flat.

12. Wake up.

13. Turn music on again.

14. Raise arms.

15. Pull left arm down with right one.

16. Massage arms.

17. Rest.

18. Think about how badly you want to look good.

19. Stand up.

20. Look in mirror.

21. "Let It Be."

Special Occasion Recipes From My Mother

WIPES

There are many different kinds of wipes. I will focus only on the ones needed in the loo. These wipes usually come in a plastic package, and the wipes stick one moist sheet on top of the next so they fit snugly into the package. This allows for a compact unit that may be placed in a small basket on the floor next to the throne.

The manufacturer does not include directions on how to get just one wipe out of the tiny package without bringing all his brothers with him. It's not that you have all day to figure this out, as you are usually in somewhat of a hurry to complete the task and scurry out of the closet.

One pulls the first wipe gently out of the package, and voilà his brother is attached, and another brother is holding on for dear life. You try to gently pull the first wipe out so as not to waste the others or allow them to dry up in your paw, but alas, seven or eight of his siblings come sliding out on your knee. This is a very uncomfortable situation, and not one where you can call for help. You very carefully push the siblings back into the package, at the same time holding onto the first one for your use. By now, all the brothers are squished into a pile, and they don't want to go back neatly into the package. You end up, therefore, with a package that looks like it has a moist ball inside, and you cannot close the sticky flap. This means that all of the wipes could dry up in seconds, and you must go purchase another supply.

Purchasing said wipes can be somewhat embarrassing. People are staring at you taking twelve of these puppies out of your cart and setting them on the conveyor belt. They are smirking, (the people, not the wipes), not only because they know why you're buying them and are aghast at the quantity in your cart, but they also know the drill of the "brothers."

Someone must have a better idea.

"Hot Spots," "Blogspots" And "Blindspots"

Over the past several months, the above terms have taken on a whole new meaning. A "hot spot" used to be a place where the temperatures were high. Now most people that go to those spots are high.

"Blogspots" are the blogs I write daily. They used to have a maximum following of 50. Recently, they have plunged to about 23, but yesterday, 143 people decided that I was the world's greatest blogger. Funny, as I wrote about how miserable I was feeling.

"Blindspots" used to be the term used when you couldn't see the moron behind you who decided to pass just as you were changing lanes. Now "blindspots" are people who are so clueless that they are called "spots," instead of humans.

"Passé!"

The following are considered "passé"

1. Cassette tapes
2. Common sense
3. corn on the cob holders
4. Compact discs
5. Savings interest rates above .03%
6. spanking (other than in the bedroom)
7. mashed potatoes
8. farting
9. the conscience
10. leaders

Booty Business

Years ago, the buttocks was not called a "booty." A "bootie," spelled more delicately, was something you put on a baby's foot. No longer. The "booty" is that part of the woman's anatomy that I spent half my life trying to hide. Now, you're not cool if it doesn't stick out far enough for someone to sit on while waiting in line. How did it get the name "booty?" Maybe from someone kicking it?

In high school, I hung out with an obese girl. She was my friend, and I never criticized her for being "fat." (It's politically incorrect to say that "f" word.) I did like walking down the street with her because her booty was four times wider than mine, so I looked quite trim next to her. I used to look in the store window reflection and chide myself because my booty wiggled up and down when I walked. Now I can't find the damned thing.

"Booty! BOOOOOOTTTTYYYYY! Where are you?" Yup. One day, I woke up, and the effen thing just disappeared. At first, I was relieved, but by this time (I was 55), the "booty" was in—the rounder and firmer, the cooler. I looked like an old woman, and I was just starting with the hot flashes. wtf. All those exercises I did for years at the gym pounding my buttocks against the wall, putting it in a canvas sling and trying to vibrate it off, were now paying off. Except, I didn't want them to. I longed for the chub, the bounce, the firm. Nope. Gone, girl.

Man's Journal (during and after the global Pandemic of 2020)

During Pandemic: (Spring 2020)

Dear Journal:

Today, I followed my usual routine: got up, ate breakfast, read paper, took dump, answered emails, prepared for second breakfast, ate second breakfast, went into morning food coma. Up from nap, groggy, as usual, heated up soup for lunch. Ate lunch with wife. Wife talks too much. Confusing. Tired. Took nap.

Up from nap, prepared to rest on the lanai (in my 'altogether'). Dozed on lanai, awakened by Mexican woman chopping palm fronds from tree next to pool. Covered 'altogether,' smiled and picked up book. Read book.

Prepared for 4:00 snack with wife. Wife talks too much. Confused. Nap before shower. Shower. Put on grill. Grill shit. Eat dinner with wife. Wife more confusing than earlier in day. Watched news. Fell asleep in third segment. Looked at emails before watching Netflix. Wife can't talk during series. Turned off TV. Went to bed. I love the wife.

After Pandemic: (Spring 2024)

Today I followed my usual routine. I will not repeat this because it's too many words, and I already wrote them once. The basic routine hasn't changed except that we have been let out of "shelter-in-place-prison." I can now play tennis, drive my sports car, go to stores without looking like a bandit, and have lunch with my guy friends. We talk about tennis, sports cars, going to stores without the bandit-look and how confusing women are.

Good News: Wife has also been let out of prison, so she is gone more, and I find her less confusing. Time for my nap.

The RBF/JWV Response: To Click Or Not To Click

During a global pandemic, if you want to actually see friends and family, Zoom or FaceTime are the main options. For those somewhat "Tech-Challenged," one must hunker down into "Googleville" and figure out how to navigate the virtual world.

After several tech tantrums, I made some fascinating discoveries, the "RBF/JWV" being the most reassuring. If one does not click the "Join With Video" option, one's "Resting Bitch Face" is not visible on the screen of participant(s). This was such a delightful discovery that I plan to forward this essay to all of my super vain friends. There is only one thing worse than someone staring at your "RBF," and that is having to look at it yourself.

Have you ever been in a Zoom meeting, your little photo is up in a corner somewhere, and you try not to look at yourself (dying at how your left eyebrow is longer and thicker than the right one) for fear someone will think you're not paying attention? But you keep sneaking a peak at yourself wishing you'd not worn that beige top that washes you out and makes you look like grass cloth. Just as you are taking that furtive glance, the host calls on you, and your face quadruples in size, as you say, "Oh, . . . yes, as you were just saying. . . "

I was in a Zoom meeting with about 40 participants when I discovered the "don't-click-it" trick. Instead of my "RBF," the others saw my professional promo photo where I'm sitting at the piano all Hoagy-like in a long green satin gown. Some guy said, "Who is that woman in the gown up there? She looks like some hooker." Well, normally, I would have defended myself, but I thought, "No, this is just a ploy to get me to show my real face, and that ain't gonna happen, fella. No RBF for you. Nope." I did not click. I do not click. I will not click.

The Arms Race

I'm getting older. There isn't much time left to get my arms in shape, so I'm working myself to a frazzle trying to get definition. Yes, at 77, I can still do this. After about eight months of daily lifting (expelling spittle that could reach Tulsa), I can now see a teeny tiny bulge in my upper arms. Of course, it could be fat settling there from the lemon pound cake I've been consuming now that Starbucks is resuming normal hours. I'm telling myself, however, it is the 150 lifts I'm doing daily that is making the difference. I'm doing this at my age because. . .

Because I can. Now some might argue that the crepe that settled on my body about eight years ago gives my age away. (Please, someone give my age away.) This will not stop me, though. I believe that if I can get enough definition in each limb, people will be so impressed with the muscle tone that they will ignore the crepe. That's a lot of crepe, I know.

In my last volume, I wrote an essay, "A Farewell to Arms." That was seven years ago when the crepe hadn't completely taken over my entire silhouette.

Since other parts of my anatomy have taken leave of their collagen, I have decided to build what little appeal I have left so as to give hope to 65-year-olds who are killing themselves at their local gyms trying to avoid this crepe crap.

Good Luck, ladies. I tried it. It didn't work. One day I woke up, and there it was staring me in the face. Looked like the paper my mom decorated the basement with for my 8th grade graduation. The crepe will come, sooner or later, so celebrate the smooth, ladies!

My muscles look great, and I will continue to lift and pull, push and punch to keep my arms in the race. I am now looking for a supersized exfoliator machine that will erase all my brown spots and bruises, permanently, s'il vous plaît. If I get bored in the meantime, I can play "connect-the-spots."

I am happy to report that my shoulders still look sexy, and my elbows haven't fallen. I can still nudge and hug, so there is hope.

Neglect-A-Size

Mr. Wonderful and I have always preferred the "full size" Bounty toweling. When I have accidentally picked up the wrong kind, he is never happy. I have been known to spend 20 minutes in front of packages ranging from flowered to white to full-size to select-a-size trying to weigh the price and advantages of each. Who does this? Didn't I have a life before Bounty. I am really BOUNTY-full.

In the middle of a global pandemic, one is not allowed to stand in front of the display for more than four seconds so one must just grab whatever is there and be thankful.

Well, Mr. Wonderful, who is meticulous to a fault, has a habit of using a piece (selected or whole) to wipe something (hopefully, not his nose) and then leave the crumpled remains somewhere on the kitchen counter. When I see it, I never know if he's trying to get his .02 worth out of it, or he just forgot to throw it away. It's usually the former. As a two-month-old witness to the Great Depression, he feels strongly that one should not be wasteful.

The other day, I heard him say, "You know, I'm getting used to this Select-a-Size thing, and I think we can deal with it." Whew. Big stress off my mind. Then I think to myself, "What about the random remains? Does this shift in taste mean that they will be smaller or easier to justify throwing them away?"

People actually spend time thinking about such things. I know.

F.Y.A.

My inner child just went on Medicare. wtf? This cannot be. I cannot be this old. I feel like I'm 25. I can still reach the steering wheel, for heavens sake. I can stay up late like the big kids and recite the Pledge of Allegro. I can still remember to say grace before an ice cream binge, and I can drink under the table any day. I really resent people making fun of my age. It's just a number after all, like 911.

I remember a colleague saying to me when I was 52, "I'll bet you were really beautiful when you were young." I wanted to say, "I'll bet you were really kind two minutes ago." What is wrong with people? At least she could have been a little passive aggressive and said, "I was just kidding!" when I gave her a dirty look.

Age is just a number, or did I say that? Hmm. My number is up; that is, it's going up way too fast. The good news is this: the older you get, the more people think you are dying, so if you are the least bit cool and active, they think you're "amazing"! At my age, people are aghast that I can stand up much less wear stilettos for three hours straight.

The worst thing you can say to an older woman is, "F.Y.A." "For your age." Are you effen kidding me? What does that mean? You can't go out after dark alone after 40? You can't travel abroad alone after menopause? Oh, and I know a lot of men have given me pause. You can't have sex after 59? Come on, people. This is the 21st century. We old farts are much more savvy than you might think. I even know how to Zoom.

I am just grateful that I still have an inner child and that Medicare is still solvent. I challenge you young chickens to keep it together when the money runs out, and you can't reach your sex toy.

Mail In Ballot: Circle Appropriate Answer

OPINION OF ESSAYS

1. HILARIOUS
2. VERY FUNNY
3. ONE OF THE ABOVE

POSTAGE REQUIRED. MUST BE POSTMARKED BY JULY 23, 2048.

The Aging Spouse

I have noticed that as the years are flying by, Mr. Wonderful has added some new, rather disconcerting behaviors to his repertoire. I am attributing them to age.

I have noticed that when I talk for more than 43 seconds, his eyes begin to flutter, and he mutters, "All of a sudden, I am incredibly tired." And off he goes to take nap #4. It is noon.

I have become aware that he doesn't answer questions I pose. If I pose more than one at a time, I might as well be talking to the toaster. He gets a puzzled look on his face, as though he's going to pass gas, and then he changes the subject. He used to say, "Not to change the subject, but. . ." He doesn't give me that courtesy anymore. I guess I'm supposed to take the hint.

I am noticing that he is spending much more time on his computer. He claims he's reading articles from erudite journals about topics I "wouldn't understand." He's right. I don't understand porn or pistons.

I realize that he no longer finds it necessary to give me a reason for his "No." He simply says, "Because." This completely shuts me down, and I'm sure that's not his intent.

His three main food groups have changed. They now include applesauce, chocolate squares and Chardonnay. The latter is not because he likes to drink; it's because he wants to sleep, and apparently, sleep is brought on by grapes as well as the fruits of my thoughts.

Final Requests

Updated list 2020-21:

1. Someone's young "C" cup boobs

2. Michele Obama's arms

3. Dr. Fauci's patience

4. Ruthie Ginsberg's grit

5. Brené Brown's wisdom

6. Sophia Loren's collagen

7. Some of Jay-Lo's buttocks

8. Yuja Wang's talent

9. Anyone's personal chef

10. A Bradley Cooper blow-up doll

11. A 20-something's female neck

12. A knee iron

WTF #2

Facetime

If I ever wanted to know just how big my nose looks on screen, or how very ugly I really look with brown spots, misplaced eye liner and crooked lips, I can just Face Time any fool who isn't afraid to "accept."

When the world is clusterf–kd, the only way we are allowed to see one another is on our screens. I haven't seen a real human whom I recognize for a minimum of three months. Actually, I didn't recognize myself the first time I broke down and face- timed someone. Fortunately, the "someone" was my daughter who swore on her naked baby photo that she would not tell anyone what I really look like.

A friend who refuses to chat on video said yesterday that she has $1600 of cheek injection credits with her plastic surgeon. The only cheeks I own that need injecting are the ones I sit on day after day looking at my feckless visage. For every minute spent exchanging boring "shelter-in-place" stories, I swear another ounce of collagen escapes into my seat cushion. This is not a good thing.

Things are even worse for me now because the accident messed up my foot, and I can't wear stilettos anymore. What does this have to do with my cheeks? It means I have to walk on the ground like the majority of you earthlings which shortens my appearance and puts more emphasis on my deflated derrière. (By the way, they don't say "derrière" for buttocks in French. It's "les fesses.") Put that in your back pocket, if it will fit.

You may be wondering how I got from face time to "fesse" time. Bonne question. No, I do not feature my "fesses" on camera, just my face. This whole thing is way too cheeky. Next.

Rule Followers

The term "rule follower" is probably foreign to some reading this. A rule follower is a person who has common sense (see footnote for definition) and does what is required for the benefit of herself and others. Rules offer direction in order to avoid chaos. Rules keep people safe. Rules have been around since before Pop Tarts.

Some people delight in bending and breaking the rules. These people don't really care about others; they are too busy trying to show others how cool they are by daring to be different and/or defiant. These people are lucky for a certain period of time, until they're not. The general rule is that if you don't follow the rules, sooner or later, you will pay the consequences.

During the recent global pandemic, the rule breakers are surfacing like zits on a boy face. Yes, most are young, but not all. There is nothing more ridiculous than watching a 70-something stick out his tongue and say, "BECAUSE! THAT'S WHY!" at a grocery store because someone asked why he wasn't wearing his mask. He needs to go home and get back in his sandbox.

Some of us follow the rules to a fault. I will not cross a street on a green light, even if it's 3 a.m. in the middle of the desert. Rules are rules. (Wtf am I doing in the desert at 3 a.m. anyway, and do they have crosswalks there?)

footnote: Common sense: Something your parents should have taught you. Google this.

New Vocabulary

During the global pandemic (Covid-19), a whole new list of vocabulary has surfaced. Here are a few of the more interesting words. Time will tell if they become mainstream or if they die with the virus.

ZOOM	A tool we use to pretend it's the same as being there.
VIRTUAL	Who knew how Zoom would bring out our worst features?
SPITTLE	Who knew you could die from a droplet? (Spit on steroids)
ASSHOLE	OBVIOUS
TESTING	I thought we were done with this in college. Turns out the test administrators may live in our own houses.
TRACING	I thought this was something you did to be a pseudo artist.

LOCKDOWN — I thought this only happened in prison. "Prison" has taken on a whole new meaning.

ISOLATION — The thing you always craved and now want no part of.

HOARDER — Never thought you'd buy all that TP, did you?

TP — Makes us think about things that never occurred to us.

SANITIZER — Makes us laugh at "Mr. Clean."

GERMAPHOBE — Who me?

EXPERT — Anyone who thinks they know more than you.

SCIENCE — That subject you got an A in but never really cared about until now.

DISTANCING — The definition of "distance" changes depending on where you're going and how fast you want to get there.

VACCINE — Something only 50% of the population will buy into. Where does this leave us?

BOOK CLUB QUESTIONS

Laudable Audible

Many people are using the versatile app, Audible, especially those who don't have time to actually sit down with a good read. (no one says "book" anymore.) The Audible app is not only practical; it's a life saver. For people who like to multi-task (no, not you, boys), you can listen while working out, walking, running, cooking, cleaning, or having boring sex.

This app is inexpensive, and you can increase your reading considerably, particularly if you have a long commute. I have quadrupled my monthly list of best sellers, and I never had to skip a beat in my daily routine. The other advantage is that when you wake up in the middle of the night and can't sleep, you can just turn that puppy on, and the story will distract your mind. Before you know it, you're zzzzing away. The bad news is when you wake up, you have missed most of what was read, and you will have no way to figure out where you left off. I have been known to reread (relisten) audible books four and five times. You won't have insomnia, though, so pick your poison.

Audible offers every kind of read from memoir to mystery, from biography to best seller, from sci-fi to YA. (Seniors, don't be mislead. YA doesn't mean "Yay." It means "Young Adult," and that's not you.)

The trick with Audible is that you must have ear buds to listen so your Mr. or Mrs. Wonderful doesn't get pissed off while he or she is trying to read the Kindle. Kindle, so passé!

Now ear buds are a whole other topic, but let it suffice to say that my ears must be deformed. I cannot get those damn little things in my head holes to save me. If I get one in, the other falls out. And the billion-dollar Apple buds, forget it. Anyone who can jog with those puppies in their ears must have some kind of suction mechanism inside their head cavity.

The narrators of these stories are often English (as in British English) readers whose voices are pleasant to the ear and make the story come alive. Some take on different roles in the stories but not all. There are even famous readers like Tom Hanks who are paid to read the author's story. I would like a stand-up to read my essays. Someone like George Carlin or Bob Hope would be perfect, but alas, they are dead, so I am left with Mrs. Maisley.

"Shelter In Place"
Calendar

2020 Colloquialisms

Really?
No, not really. I just said "really," I didn't mean "really;" I meant something else. But what else could I have meant? Isn't "really" a bit superfluous? Yeah, but it is what it is.

What can you do?
I don't know. What can you do? Why are you asking me? What do you mean, you don't expect a response. Why ask a question, if you don't want a response? Which "you" are you referring to? Me? Who?

Are you kidding me?
Well, I might be, but that's for you to decide. What do you mean, you didn't really mean it literally? Then how did you mean it? It's an "expression?" An "expression" that requires no response? What's so funny about that?

Take care.
Take it where? What's care? Where do you get some? I don't really care.

Good Grief!
What's good about grief? I thought grief was sad. How can something good be sad? This makes no sense.

Here's the Bottom Line
Where is the bottom? Whose bottom is it? And why would there be a line on someone's bottom? This makes no sense. I already said that.

That's that!
That's what? What is that? "That is that," you say? But if that's not that, would you say, "That's not that?"

Binge watch
Haven't been a binger since 1956 when I binged on Fudge Royal ice cream. Yup. I usually took in about 1/2 gallon at a time before rushing to sit in front of American Bandstand. "Binge" watching is the practice of watching multiple episodes of a given TV program at a time. I am willing to bet that those who do this are not sitting with idle mouths. I would guess that they are probably consuming at least a pound of sugar or salt in the process, with a likelihood of serious alcohol to wash it down. Really? Well, I guess it is what it is.

Tweet
A signature of the present commander in chief. He is a very strange bird whose songs do not necessarily resonate with global big birds.

WOTY (Word of the Year)
What is your word of the year? Is there a word that you keep hearing yourself say? It may be a phrase, not just a single word. Bottom Line: My favorites are inappropriate for this tome.

I Could Care Less
Well, if you could, why don't you? If you care less, what does that mean? Did you care a lot or just a little to begin with? If you only cared a little, then you probably don't care at all, so why bother saying anything? If you could care less, but you don't care less, then you must care more, right? That's that.

Not a Happy Camper
A camper can be a person or a kind of trailer. If it's a trailer, how can it be happy? How does one know if it's happy? It can't talk, and it has no emojis at its disposal to let us know how happy it is. Would you be happy being dragged around the country filled with stale baked bean odor and sweaty deer hunters? If the definition refers to a person, then a camper's happiness would depend on many things: the weather, the distance traveled, the condition of the camping grounds' port-apotties, the mosquito index. How could anyone really be "happy" in any of these situations? I don't get it. But what can you do?

I Hear You

Why wouldn't you hear me, and why do you feel it necessary to tell me you hear me. If you respond, I already know you've heard me. Do you say, "I see you!" too? Everyone knows that men only hear when we women are whispering; otherwise, they say they never heard us say anything. Women hear everything, and we remember it for decades.